Marketing for the
Voluntary Sector

Marketing for the Voluntary Sector

A GUIDE TO MEASURING MARKETING PERFORMANCE

EDITED BY **PAULA KEAVENEY**
AND **MICHAEL KAUFMANN**

IN ASSOCIATION WITH
Marketing

KOGAN PAGE

First published in 2001

Kogan Page Limited
120 Pentonville Road
London
N1 9JN
UK

Kogan Page Limited
163 Central Avenue, Suite 2
Dover
NH 03820
USA

British Library Cataloguing in Publication Data

A CIP record for this book is available from the British Library.

ISBN 0 7494 3250 0

Typeset by Jean Cussons Typesetting, Diss, Norfolk
Printed and bound in Great Britain by Clays Ltd, St Ives plc

Contents

List of contributors   *vii*
Foreword   *xi*

Introduction   **1**

Part 1: Who are we?

1. The charity brand and its identity – who you are
    and what you do
    Paula Keaveney   · 7

2. Marketing within the organizational structure
    Michael Kaufmann   18

Part 2: Who are our customers?

3. Marketing to donors
    Paula Keaveney   29

4. Marketing to opinion formers – political
    communications in the voluntary sector
    David Hughes   34

Part 3: Tools and techniques

5. Marketing on the Internet
    Paula Keaveney and Mike Ward   49

6. Relationship marketing and membership schemes
    Susan Kay-Williams   58

7. Partnerships with companies
    David Pettigrew   68

8. PR-led marketing communications
    Olly Grender   84

9. Events and conferences as a marketing tool
    Howard Barclay   96

10. Annual reports as marketing tools
    Veronica Crichton   110

11. Evaluation tools and techniques
    Mark Westaby and Peter Crowe   119

12. Integrated campaigning
    Neil Churchill   129

13. Advertising
    Paula Keaveney   148

14. Database marketing for voluntary organizations
    – databases and why they matter
    Peter Larsen   156

Appendix 1 Further reading   166
Appendix 2 Useful organizational contacts   170

Index   173

List of contributors

Howard Barclay is a freelance events specialist and the owner of Jigsaw Communications. He has worked on projects for a range of charities including Scope, Leonard Cheshire and the Muscular Dystrophy Campaign.

Neil Churchill is Deputy Chief Executive of Crisis, the national charity for homeless people. His brief includes the whole range of campaigning activity, from government affairs and media relations through to marketing and fundraising. Neil was previously Head of Communications at Barnardo's and at the Policy Studies Institute. He managed media relations for the 150th birthday of Thomas Barnardo. This won the *PR Week* and IPR awards for best charity campaign. He is a trustee of Alone in London.

Veronica Crichton is a journalist by trade who has run her own business for the past 19 years. Much of her work is as a copywriter for a wide range of organizations in the private, public and voluntary sectors.

Peter Crowe is a freelance marketing and PR consultant. He has worked for the National Dairy Council as both Publicity Manager and Marketing Manager. Prior to joining the NDC, he spent nine years in various roles at the Health Education Council. Peter has made a particular study of the application of planning and evaluation techniques to PR, and has recently been instrumental in developing the ConsumerPulse planning software for leading planning and evaluation consultancy, Metrica. He is a member of the Marketing Society and the Institute of Public Relations, and he is also a member and past Chairman of the organizing committee for the IPR Marketing Communications Group.

Olly Grender is a director of LLM Communications. She joined the company in 1999 and runs the Strategic Communications Unit. She was formerly Director of Communications at Shelter, heading a 40-strong department responsible for policy, media, public affairs and publications. Before that, Olly worked for the Liberal Democrats for five years, having previously been a researcher and speechwriter for Paddy Ashdown.

David Hughes has worked in political and corporate communications for more than 15 years, advising well-known companies, trade associations and statutory bodies, as well as organizations in the voluntary sector, including the Royal Society for the Protection of Animals (RSPCA). His other clients have included Cambridge University, Toyota, Granada Television, Goldman Sachs, the Crown Estates and a number of companies in the energy and construction sectors.

Michael Kaufmann has been a design director for major publishing houses and national newspapers. A former assistant director (Marketing and Communications) for NCH Action for Children, he works as a freelance journalist and as a consultant to organizations within the not-for-profit sector.

Susan Kay-Williams is Head of Marketing and External Relations for the Guide Association, the largest voluntary organization for girls and young women in the UK. She has previously worked for the British Lung Foundation, United World Colleges and Burnett Associates and on several arts marketing projects, with responsibility for marketing development and for fundraising from individuals and organizations worldwide. She has recently been awarded her PhD on the development of fundraising and the use of marketing in charities and has presented papers in the UK and USA on relationship building for fundraising.

Paula Keaveney is a specialist in marketing and communications for charities. She has been Head of Communications at the Muscular Dystrophy Campaign and Head of Media and PR at NCH Action for Children. A former BBC journalist, Paula has also worked for the Save the Children Fund, the Refugee Council and Autism Initiatives. She is a winner of the Charity Publication of the Year award, a trustee of the Muscular Dystrophy Campaign and a member of the Institute of Public Relations.

Peter Larsen is a marketing systems and information specialist. He is Managing Director of Phrasis KBDM, who supply consultancy, analytic and database solutions to a wide range of organizations. During his time as Marketing Database Manager of Greenpeace, Peter designed and delivered a new supporter database using microcomputer technology that reduced annual running costs by over £250,000. Applying technology to marketing and communications processes as the service provider, consultant and end client for 14 years has given him a unique perspective on successful solution delivery.

David Pettigrew is a corporate fundraising specialist who works in Australia. He was formerly Head of Corporate Fundraising for NCH Action for Children Scotland.

Mike Ward is Principal Lecturer in Journalism at the University of Central Lancashire in Preston. A former BBC journalist, he is the course leader of the MA in online journalism at the university's nationally recognized Department of Journalism. His book *Journalism Online: How to create effective Web content* will be published in 2001. He has also provided media relations consultancy for several charities.

Mark Westaby is Director of Portfolio Communications and Managing Director of Metrica. Previously a director of Countrywide Communications and a senior consultant at Kinnear, he worked as a consulting engineer before moving into PR. He has broad experience in international marketing communication for leading IT companies and industrial organizations. Mark specializes in communication measurement, planning and research, and he developed the Metrica media analysis system, Cigma, which is

Foreword

I have been fortunate to have had a great deal of involvement with the voluntary sector – as a chief executive, and a trustee, and sometimes as chair – both at local and at national level. Voluntary organizations are crucial to any democratic society. I recall visiting some Eastern European countries after the fall of communism and discussing with them the establishment of voluntary organizations as part of civic society.

I spent some two and a half years in Northern Ireland where there is a very successful and vibrant voluntary sector, often involved in working for reconciliation between the communities and sometimes very active in lessening tensions.

I have also been involved with the voluntary sector through being an elected local councillor and an MP. I know the importance of understanding the market, of communicating clearly and of getting the message right. Charities are now a highly professional business with a real cutting edge. They have to be efficient, and demonstrate value for money in achieving their objectives. They must do this without neglecting their other strengths of having a sound base in their local or national communities and being experimental and exciting in their work.

Those that do not do this will lag behind and lose opportunities to gain support, improve services, influence the political system and raise funds.

This book argues that an understanding of marketing must be at the heart of every successful charity. The book does more than argue though; it also provides guidance and examples for charities wanting to improve their marketing. I am sure it will prove invaluable to those working in the voluntary sector and to all those who want to understand it better.

Lord Alf Dubs

Alf Dubs is a Labour working peer, was a Northern Ireland Office minister from May 1997 to December 1999 and was the MP for Battersea (in London) until 1987. He has been Director of the Refugee Council, a trustee of Action and One World Action, Chair of the Nicaragua Health Fund, Liberty and the Fabian Society and has been associated with several other national and local voluntary organizations. In the run-up to the 1992 general election, he chaired a Labour Party working group developing policies for the voluntary sector.

Introduction

Paula Keaveney and Michael Kaufmann

When Doctor Barnardo helped find homes for street children and started a series of orphanages, he would not have realized he was in marketing. Driven by philanthropy and faith, he and his supporters were doing what they saw as right. Yet, in today's terms he was a classic marketer – spotting an unmet need and attempting to fill the gap. The difference for the good doctor, of course, was that his primary customers – the children – could not pay. He had to find secondary customers, supporters and donors, who could meet the financial demands.

Much the same is true today. Most voluntary organizations have distinct groupings of customers. Meeting groups' needs while maintaining a strong sense of purpose and mission is the main challenge facing charities today.

This book is about who those customers might be, and about ways of meeting their needs. We assume that charities already know enough about their goals and mission not to be blown totally off course.

The charity world in the United Kingdom is huge. The Charity Commission registers up to 50 new organizations each month. Charities range from massive international concerns to tiny community groups dependent on volunteers. Many charity staff or volunteers have a marketing role, even if they do not realize it.

Speak to most staff and volunteers, however, and they will deny they are in marketing. They will tell you they are helpers, are providing a service or are carrying out a specific operational task. Yet, by delivering the product – whether it be a service, a fundraising relationship, a lobbying idea, or even a building, they are in marketing. This book argues that if an organization is to succeed in its goals, a marketing approach should permeate right the way through, from top to bottom.

Yet, there is a reluctance in many organizations. Some readers, for example, may already be reacting to the use of the word customer in this introduction. It is quite deliberate. Customers, whether organizations or individuals, have choice and influence. Donors, local authorities, opinion formers, the media, all have the choice of whether or not to support a particular charity. They also, through exercising that choice, have influence and through exercise of that influence can change parts of what the charity does. They make up the markets within which the charity operates. Without knowledge and understanding of those markets, the charity, quite simply, will fail.

That does not mean charities operate in a value-free vacuum; rather that by knowing themselves and their mission, and by knowing the markets they exist to serve or work in, charities can match their activities to external needs and make sure that they achieve as much as possible for their beneficiaries.

If marketing is so important then, why does it permeate so few charities? Much of the answer is to be found in history. Organizations founded to meet specific needs can soon have huge operational infrastructures that then lead future strategy. (Structural issues are addressed in Part 1, Chapter 2.) Life then revolves around the product. This is fine as long as demand remains. But social provision can have a product life cycle in the same way that a car or a piece of consumer hardware does. Take orphanages. There was a time in the nineteenth century when fashion favoured large institutions for children on their own. Since then opinion has moved on. An organization wanting to provide orphanages to this extent today would quite simply go out of business. This is not to denigrate those running the operational side of charities. The product, and its quality, will always be key. In fact adopting a marketing approach throughout an organization should enhance the status of those delivering the charity's services.

The marketing approach has been more readily adopted in fundraising departments, which today operate in an increasingly competitive environment. Donors to charities are no longer seen as an amorphous mass, but as groups of individuals or organizations with varying needs and interests. An individual donor could give a one-off gift and not want any information at all, or subscribe to a child sponsorship scheme in which individual letters from an individual child meet the need for personal contact and commitment. (Fundraising is covered in general in Part 2, Chapter 3, and in detail in a number of chapters in Part 3.)

As the environment in which charities operate becomes ever more competitive, the need for organizations to make themselves distinct, to stand out from the crowd, becomes increasingly pressing. In the same way that commercial organizations seek to define themselves and what they offer, charities have taken on the need for clear branding and positioning – for knowing who they are and where they are going. In the charity world, this can be an area of great conflict and complexity. Profile raising can demand attention focused on relatively minor aspects of the whole charity's work, with public perception differing greatly from the reality of the charity involved.

There is any number of textbooks on the theory of marketing, and the authors have recommended and listed some of these in an appendix to this book. Our objective is to provide a guide for readers wanting to think about their organization's identity and branding, to look at its markets, to plan its marketing and then to get out there and do it. Chapters are written by authors with specific knowledge and experience of their subjects. These contributors are drawn from a range of charities and agencies. A wide range of sections of the charity world is covered, in many cases through examples and case studies.

This book divides into three parts. Part 1 looks at aspects of the charity's nature, including branding, identity and whether marketing is integrated into its structure. Part 2 looks at markets and focuses on funders and opinion formers. Part 3, the lengthiest part of this book, looks at marketing tools and techniques. It also focuses on how to integrate activities, and how to evaluate and plan.

The appendices contain suggestions for further reading and a list of useful organizations.

While many authors have experience of large charities, all the topics covered contain lessons for small and medium-sized groups too. In fact, it is more important that staff, volunteers and trustees in smaller organizations understand marketing issues, as they are less likely to have the resources to allow occasional failure.

Marketing is about meeting needs. Charities exist to meet needs. Organizations that understand marketing, and which have a real understanding of their markets and customers, will be more able to do the work they were set up to do.

Part 1

Who are we?

This section looks at the branding, positioning and marketing structures in voluntary organizations.

1

The charity brand and its identity – who you are and what you do

Paula Keaveney

The origin of the popular use of the word 'brand' comes from the world of the Wild West. When great herds of cattle were kept on massive ranges, and were driven across country for sale, it was important to know who owned which animal. Cattle were branded with distinctive marks. Branding then was little more than a sign of origin and was, in fact, very similar to slapping a logo on a product.

Since then, the meaning of the word brand has undergone a re-brand itself. The verbs to brand and to re-brand have become common in discussion. Brands have become both very valuable, with companies adding sums to their annual accounts to represent the value of their brand, and very superficial, with every change of appearance being referred to as a new brand.

Not surprisingly, there is now huge confusion about the meaning of the word, with other phrases being used interchangeably. Readers interested in definitions will find many marketing textbooks looking at this issue. For the purposes of this chapter, however, the word brand refers to who you are and what you do – in other words to the nature and essence of your charity and how that is understood.

For anyone running a small charity, struggling to raise money and simply keep going, the issue of branding may seem esoteric and unnecessary. Yet, if you are not clear about the nature of your organization and its reason for existence, you might find maintaining that existence becoming more and more difficult. And if you do not know what you are, how can you work out where you are, or where you should be going?

The nature of an organization permeates every aspect of its operations whether we want it to or not. To understand this, think of the number of decisions that a charity may need to make. What type of staff are you going to recruit; what should your reception look or feel like; are your trustees users of the service or dispassionate supporters; what is the atmosphere like within the charity; how do you answer the phone; and so on. In a typical week, you are likely to be making many decisions (whether consciously or not) that will be influenced by the brand. If the nature of your charity is unclear, these decisions are likely to feel unguided, random or unnecessarily difficult.

The need for clarity in decisions is itself an excellent reason for looking at your brand.

REASONS TO LOOK AT THE CHARITY'S BRAND

This can be due to the following:

■ the circumstances have changed;
■ the mission of the charity seems misleading;
■ the mission of the charity relates to historical fact;
■ key people within the charity seem uncertain of why it exists;
■ the wider public seems uncertain of why the charity exists;
■ internal change means there is a desire to look at basics;
■ there is a need for team and morale building.

There is plenty of advice about how to look at and understand what your brand is and what it should be. Much of this advice involves trying to give your charity a personality (called a brand personality). There are many types of exercises you can do. You can compare the organization to an animal, to a historical figure, to a car and so on. You can invite board members away for weekend strategy sessions, you can carry out structured or semi-structured interviews with clients, you can run focus groups with staff. The techniques you use will depend very much on the nature of your organization.

HOW TO THINK ABOUT BRANDING

▨ Start with your mission statement and charity objects.
▨ Read up on how and why the charity was founded.
▨ Analyse what might have changed both internally and exter-
  nally.
▨ Get people to sum up the charity in a word or a phrase.
▨ Justify to yourself your current range of activities.
▨ List which activities you would not ever carry out, and ask
  yourself why.

The process of thinking about branding is one in which your charity is likely to have little expertise. By definition, it is not a regular occurrence. It is well worth doing some preliminary research to find a charity of a similar size to yours that has been through such an exercise. Questioning those involved in a similar process is likely to save you time and money in your own work. Many of the organizations listed in Appendix 2 of this book will be able to suggest leads and possible contacts. Larger charities tend to document their process and to be willing to spend time discussing it with colleagues from the sector.

Researching re-branding

Organizations to ask include:

▨ Scope (formerly the Spastics Society);
▨ Voluntary Service Overseas;
▨ The Media Trust;
▨ The National Council for Voluntary Organisations.

As already discussed, a charity's brand is about much more than what the organization looks or sounds like. It is about its essence, about all the associated thoughts and feelings. Being clear about who you are is vital. But, once you have defined this, you need to decide how to communicate it. This means looking at what you communicate now and how different that is from your reality. Some difference will always exist. But too much difference means it may be time to look again at how your image reflects your identity.

It is always worth reflecting on whether image and identity match. This should involve gathering the thoughts and perceptions of individuals in key audiences or markets. Not every charity will want, or need, to make changes. However, the bulk of this chapter is devoted to the issues involved when deciding on, and implementing change.

WHAT IS IN A NAME?

The importance of a name cannot be overstated. All charities communicate in more ways than they realize – printed materials, videos, letters, the way the receptionist answers the telephone and even the franking on envelopes. What all these have in common is the name of the charity. Whatever other messages are conveyed, the name remains common. Clearly, having a misleading or difficult name can ruin the efforts of all involved.

Closely associated with the charity name is its logo. Tied up with both is the general approach to appearance or visual identity. The 1990s saw a plethora of charities changing their name, logo or look. In some cases, this was promoted by a very real change in the nature of the organization. Perhaps the best-known example of this is the charity Scope, which used to be called the Spastics Society. Other changes are motivated by a more general feeling that there is a need to be sharper, more modern and so on. While these may be worthy reasons to take some action, they are not enough justification to go through the lengthy and often difficult process of a change. The only justification should be that the name or image no longer communicates the reality of the charity, its mission and its approach.

Examples of changes

In 1990, the British Refugee Council changed its name to the Refugee Council. In 1999, the Muscular Dystrophy Group of Great Britain and Northern Ireland changed its name to the Muscular Dystrophy Campaign. In 2000, the British Diabetic Association changed its name to Diabetes UK.

NAMING

Getting the name right is vital. Yet, names are often chosen because of a consultative process yielding unworkable compromises. It is worth accepting at the very beginning of the process that a name will never be able to sum up absolutely everything the charity does. It should instead aim to sum up the core mission. Save the Children, for example, also works with young people and adults but would not dream of adding a list to its name. The Muscular Dystrophy Campaign also funds research into medical conditions that are not, strictly speaking, muscular dystrophy. It would, however, have a very difficult name to use if it became the 'Muscular Dystrophy and allied neuromuscular conditions campaign'.

Core mission is essential. But so is workability. It is quite possible to choose a name that sums up the heart of the charity but is still unworkable. Names need to work on paper and in conversation. Clever phrases that are difficult to pronounce will be mispronounced or abbreviated. It is important to remember that once a name is in the outside world, it is shared property. If those who are meant to use it cannot or would not, the charity has a problem. Phrases that appear to conflict with basic grammar or with the way people normally read or speak, will fail. This does not mean ruling out creativity. 'Whizz Kidz' works, for example.

Many chapters of this book will argue that consistency and repetition are vital in marketing. And so they are if the charity is to get its message across. But if this is the case, why cannot names be enforced with enough advertising, persistence and internal guidelines? Why cannot names be made workable by force of effort? Unfortunately, life and common-sense experience tell us this is not so. Language belongs to those who use it. This is easily understood by thinking about some very common brand names and the way their use has become widespread. There may be no Hoover models in the local hardware shop, but most people going in to buy a vacuum cleaner will probably refer to it as a Hoover. The word has come to be owned by the speakers in a way that no amount of guidelines will prevent.

WORKABILITY TRAPS

Writers, and especially journalists, are taught to spell out the words indicated by initials before using the shorter version. Names based on initials will get this treatment. Choosing initial-based names is always a big risk.

A lot of time can be wasted trying to enforce the use of lowercase or uppercase letters. If the basic rules of English contradict what you are trying to do, the name may not be workable.

Unless you write a huge amount of letters, the name is likely to be spoken more often than it is written. If it is too long, or difficult to say, it will be mangled.

LOGOS

In many cases, a new name will mean a new logo. The name, logo and core colours need to work together to reinforce your brand image.

The rules for logo choice are similar to those for names. It is important to accept that a logo cannot represent everything the charity does. At one time there was a rash of logos that tried to combine too many elements – a black hand and a white hand holding a globe while a bird of peace flew by is a fictitious example, but not too far from the truth.

Logos should be designed to be memorable, to have impact and to be reproducible. A common mistake made by charities is to choose an attractive logo that looks brilliant on a designer's PowerPoint presentation, but which will not work on the photo-copier.

Repetition builds brand image. The logo therefore must work on everything if the charity is to achieve that repetition. In some cases, charities will make heavy use of branded T-shirts. In others, banners will be important. In every case, however, charities need to think about the full range of their communications vehicles (and that may well include real vehicles) before settling on a logo.

MAKING A CHANGE WORK

Introducing change can be slow and difficult. How a new logo and name are chosen, introduced and communicated can make all the difference between success and failure. As a rule of thumb, the internal communications process needed before the change 'goes live' will take at least twice as long as the choice process. Whereas head office staff can be spoken to, sent a memo or e-mailed on a daily basis, branch supporters scattered throughout the country will take longer to be kept informed. Particular groups will be used to particular methods of communication. Supporters who mainly get information through meetings will need to be kept informed that way. A sudden change to letters is likely to be counterproductive.

Introducing a new name and logo involves a balance between friendly persuasion and simple rules. People will have different concerns. Some will want to discuss the rationale for the change; others will want to know how the new logo will work on their jumble sale leaflet. This is where house style guidelines come into their own. Once a logo, name and style are chosen, a simple document showing how the logo and name should and should not be used is a vital tool in both persuading and ensuring consistency.

This might simply address the look of the charity and its publications. Or it might fit into a broader style guide or corporate identity manual that covers use of language, photography and so on. Any charity embarking on a change would be well advised to look at different versions of these publications produced by charities that have given thought to their corporate image.

HOW TO DO IT?

Few charities will have experience of going through this process. Staff and trustees may feel uncertain about how to go about it.

There are plenty of outside agencies that can provide a partial or full service for you – from early discussions to the production of logo and style guide. The benefits of external help include the valuable outside perspective and the ability to gain advice untainted by internal politics. There is, however, no reason why this cannot also be done in-house. The benefits of an in-house process include time saved on briefings and staff with knowledge of the outputs required.

Whichever process is used, it will not work unless:

▩ a senior member of staff steers it through with little interference;

▩ the reason for the change is defined clearly at the start of the project;

▩ enough time is left for idea generation, sign offs, printing and the essential sell-in process.

At some point, the charity will want to adopt the new name officially at an AGM or equivalent meeting. It will also need to register the name with the Charity Commission and with Companies House if the organization is also a registered company. It is possible to begin using the new name before this process has been carried out, as long as the old name is used as well. The old name need not be prominent. Phrases such as 'registered as XX' or 'formerly the XX' can be useful. It is worth taking legal advice if you are unsure about what needs to appear on a letterhead in the changeover period.

BENEFIT BY-PRODUCTS

Often the most beneficial effect a change of visual identity can have is that of a catalyst for consistency. By the time charities change, they can have a range of publications and other products that, because of different designers or authors, do not bear much resemblance to one another. Instead of reinforcing one another, the appearance of these products means that they fight with one another and confuse the reader or viewer. A change of name and logo forces the organization to rewrite and redesign. This can mean that, for the first time, materials look as if they come from the same organization. Repetition and reinforcement become possible. It is worth bearing this in mind when weighing up the costs and benefits of a change.

BRANDING AND CORPORATE ID

British Diabetic Association to Diabetes UK (case study by Vanessa Hebditch)

2000

Diabetes UK (formerly the British Diabetic Association) is the United Kingdom's largest charity for people with diabetes. Founded in 1934, the Association's identity had become confused. There were problems with meaning linked to problems with profile. This lack of clarity was reflected in its visual identity, with a profusion of logos and styles being used. Over a period of five years, the Association reviewed its brand. In June 2000, the Association changed its corporate identity and name to Diabetes UK.

1995/96

The issue of identity was first raised by the staff management group. A survey of the Association's members and questionnaires and sessions at the Association's conference for volunteers both showed a need and desire for a stronger, clearer image.

1997

Further research was carried out – a Mori poll (general public) and small focus groups (the diabetes community, including people with diabetes, their carers and healthcare professionals). The charity is seen as authoritative and caring but also old-fashioned and not dynamic. The research highlights a desire for a higher profile – both for the condition and the organization; for a 'symbol' of diabetes; and for clarity in the organization's aims.

April 1998
A brief is written. Four consultancies are chosen to pitch for the work. Fishburn Hedges (FH) is appointed.

June–July 1998
FH carries out a communications audit and consultation among key stakeholders. Although a change of name had not been part of the original brief, the consultation process shows a need to look at the name.

August 1998
Review of strategic plan.

September 1998
Presentation to Board of Trustees outlining the results of consultation with a number of options for the way forward.

December 1998
Board of Trustees ratified the strategic plans for the Association, the name change and delegates authority for agreeing the final designs to a small working group. Launch date of June 2000 confirmed.

January–March 1999
Complete audit of the Association's communication materials undertaken. This involves identifying all items that need to be changed, weeding out any duplication and agreeing any new items. Schedule produced for the running down of existing materials so that any wastage is minimized. An implementation timescale for producing and printing all items is produced.

February 1999
Logo design brief agreed.

March 1999
Three potential design routes chosen for further development.

April 1999
Board of Trustees and staff day-long meeting on the mission, vision and values. Chosen design route developed with work

carried out on the different elements such as the style, colour and typography.

May 1999
Agreement of final design of new logo. Work begins on complete set of detailed house style guidelines.

June 1999
A full internal communication programme is drawn up involving mailings, articles in internal publications, seminars, talks and conferences to all internal audiences from staff to members, volunteers and healthcare professionals.

November 1999
External communication plan agreed including mailings of materials, PR and media plans and advertising brief.

February 2000
Production of all promotional and fundraising materials completed. Internal launch to volunteers.

March 2000
Internal launch to healthcare professional members.

April 2000
All stationery and core leaflets completed.

May 2000
Staff briefing seminars held on new guidelines for use of identity.

June 2000
Launch to wider membership and public.

July 2000
Ongoing PR work, roll out of new design on any other existing materials as stocks run down.

2

Marketing within the organizational structure

Michael Kaufmann

Marketing within voluntary organizations is very much a child of
the late 1990s. It is surprising how quickly the professional cadres
have sprung full fledged and experienced to the fore. Of course,
those larger agencies whose primary objective was raising awareness through campaigning, or the raising of funds through awareness, have long been well versed in marketing. It has been those
charities whose primary objective is the actual delivery of succour
and care to the young, the old and the socially excluded that have
been the tardiest in embracing marketing. However, with the
variety of charities and agencies within the sector, the ideal
marketing structure within each will vary accordingly.

The following case history shows how, as awareness of
marketing as a valuable tool for increasing profile within both the
client user base and donors grew, one large charity changed its
internal structure to accommodate it.

CASE HISTORY

In early 1994, after 125 years of existence, NCH Action for Children had just changed its name and corporate identity and had become aware of 'brand' (see Chapter 1). NCH then had over 200 projects largely funded from statutory sources. It was thus operationally led and displayed some suspicions of the terminology of marketing and the word itself. The internal structure, simplified here, was loosely as shown in Figure 2.1.

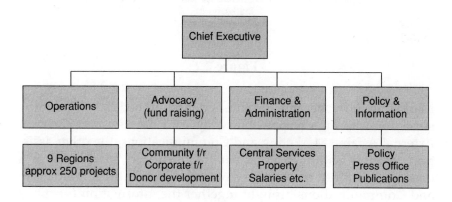

Figure 2.1

The concept of 'marketing' was raised within Policy & Information and by a Regional Director of Social Work. On the initiative of the Director of Policy & Information there followed the inevitable meeting with consultants. A report was produced after interviews across the breadth of NCH. It met the predictable culture clash and was thought to be incompatible with operational values and sensitivities.

There the initiative may have ended but for a change of personnel. A new director arrived and 'advocacy' became 'fundraising'. This individual had a solid grounding in marketing and the internal culture started to shift. Shortly, the Director of Policy & Information left to take over the helm of another agency and the structure of the organization underwent a sea change (see Figure 2.2).

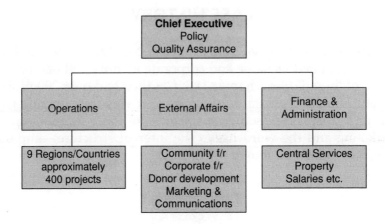

Figure 2.2

Marketing now became established and imbedded within the structure. Although responsibility lay with the Assistant Director, External Affairs, Marketing and Communications, the other assistant directors within External Affairs all carried 'Marketing' as a descriptor in their now clumsy but effective job titles. Marketing and Communications brought together the information functions of Press & PR and the Publications Department with the old 'advocacy' functions of Events and the Celebrity team.

But of course, as ever with a childcare charity working largely within the statutory sector, a great deal of marketing lay within the remit of Operational Directors of Social Work. Marketing of the agency to local authorities has long been the real key to NCH's success and rapid growth. Marketing to the statutory sector is discussed later.

While this latter growth continued apace, and the agency was well known and respected within the social work sphere, market research showed there was little recognition of NCH within the general populace. The urgent need for donors to fill the shortfall between statutory provision and excellent service delivery became more crucial as the agency grew.

So, new structures are in place, a new century is underway, and there exists the prime opportunity for marketers to prove their worth to those parts of the voluntary sector that are not saving animals. Watch this space.

SMALLER ORGANIZATIONS

Organizations depend on the public perception of what they do to a greater or lesser degree. Ask any of Britain's rough sleepers and they will confirm that begging in a sea of beggars is a soul destroying process. Awareness of the tools and techniques of marketing, as outlined elsewhere in this book, is indispensable. But this is an awareness that needs imbedding within the organizational culture. The problem arises for smaller charities, without the bureaucracy and staffing levels that can accommodate a marketing function within the official structure, of where and with whom the responsibility lies.

The answer, as ever, lies within planning. All agencies, commercial or voluntary, survive on their ability to plan the strategy that will deliver their objectives and avoid potential pitfalls. It is here that marketing should be considered as the tactical plan, an integral part of the mechanism to achieve this. However, the possibility that the required expertise exists within the workforce of a small charity is an unlikely one. It is here where the services of a marketing consultant should be considered.

WORKING WITH CONSULTANTS

Why consultants?

As the third sector has evolved, it is no longer enough to do good with good intentions. Voluntary organizations are now more outcome focused with growing emphasis on best practice and best value. They now need to be responsible for what they do and how they do it. The 'why', the motivation, is now taken as read although it remains for too many the basis on which they raise funds. As there has been a shift from the 'why', to the 'what' and the 'how', we witness the shift from process to product, to achievement, or outcomes.

Process

This shift has made consultants a part of the pattern of change. Organizations recognize the shift and most are now process focused. It is those very processes, the lifeblood of bureaucracy, which can paralyse organizations and lead to decisions based on how things will be done, not on what should be done. Flexibility has now become an organizational catchword, even a cliché. Despite it being an essential criterion for job selection, its actuality is still far from universal. Pre-ordained processes are safe, they have become an excuse for failure. Process has thus become more important than product.

Decision making

Knowledge of colleagues and their reactions, the subtle tones of internal politics, can limit an organization's ability to make decisions. The implementation process influences what decisions look like and, more often, what they do not look like. Committees, boards or other inclusive management structures are not ideal forums for incisive decision making. What they do is present arguments for or against. Often the committee designs the proverbial camel. One person, by virtue of his or her job title, then endorses that design and calls it a decision.

Enter the consultant

Just as charities are becoming more responsible for their outcomes, so they should be holding their consultants responsible for their input. But there is a tendency to give the consultant every reason why his or her advice would not work. Internal processes distort the outcome and nullify advice. This does not disenchant them with the consultant. Everybody feels safer with someone else to blame. Many people working in charities hide behind the fact that, because they do good, they must be doing it right. This is not always a conscious process.

To use your consultant well it is crucial to recognize that the expertise required to implement successful change is not something that you have on your payroll, year in, year out. Consultants are not hard to find – check your waste bin for mail shots or ask around. Get a few to pitch competitively for whatever you have in mind. If they cannot sell themselves, they cannot sell you. But do not seek to take advantage of them. Word gets about, your reputation will be damaged and the good ones will shun you. There is the example of an unnamed organization that asked a consultant to analyse and report on the problems it was having with fundraising, and present the report as a pitch for the work in changing this. The consultant produced a considered report that was somewhat embarrassing for the recipients. Faults in process were highlighted. Marketing was identified as weak. Solutions were proposed. Silence ensued. The consultant was promised a response that never came. The Greeks have a word for it. So do I, but decorum forbids.

You must not impose artificial restrictions on the outcomes by dictating process. Explain your objectives, demonstrate your structures, be open about budgets, explain your ethical codes – and then trust your choice of consultant.

Do not pre-conceive the outcome or you will most certainly be disappointed. It is strange how many people do this. It is tantamount to using your consultant as an over-paid design mechanic. If you dictate the outcome, you are only buying process – and that is something you get from a management consultant, not a marketing and communications expert.

Do not make the outcome subject to an internal beauty contest. If you are happy with the outcome, ride your judgement. Do not ask internal staff to vote on it – sell it to them!

Do not accept work that you have doubts about. If you are unhappy with the outcome, do not try to improve it. Any result would be a compromise. Georgian porticos look silly on bungalows. Send the consultant away to do better. If they cannot, get yourself another consultant and do not pay the first their full fee.

Let one person manage the relationship. In a larger charity, the director of marketing, head of communications or similar post should have responsibility for working with the consultancy. That should not exclude advice and support from colleagues. But senior directors and chief executives should not deal with consultants over the head of the responsible person. Consultants love nothing better than access as high as possible up the corporate ladder where it gets very difficult to work out who is carrying the can. It is amazing how often senior executives can be flattered into bad positions by persuasive consultants with an idea to sell. In a small charity, the relationship is usually best handled by the person responsible for fundraising.

It should be remembered that a good marketing strategy is not about personal 'likes' and 'dislikes'. A senior executive or chairperson may well say 'I don't like it – can't stand green'. Such statements, which staff members feel unable to challenge, are common. Of course, green will turn out to be the colour of the car that squashed the chairperson's pet dog. It is not about taste or even aesthetics; it is about effective communications.

Pay for what you get and get what you pay for. Remember, only you can devalue the deal. It is a buyer's market, however posh and intimidating your consultant may pretend to be.

In summary, some dos and don'ts when working with a marketing consultant:

- Recognize expertise.
- Do not dictate process.
- Do not preconceive outcomes.
- Let one person manage the relationship.
- Support that person.
- Do not let outcomes become subject to an internal popularity contest.
- Do not let individuals prejudice the outcome.
- Do not accept work with which you are unhappy.
- Pay for what you get.

MARKETING TO THE STATUTORY SECTOR

The growth of statutory work undertaken by both commercial and charitable organizations in the UK from 1980–2000 has both mirrored and been largely responsible for the growth in voluntary organizations *per se*. Driven by the Thatcher Government's privatization plans and policy of limiting the remit of local government, this phenomenon has created a massive change in the way charities both fund and market themselves. The crop of scandals surrounding both local authority and charitable care seems not to have caused great or lasting damage to the reputation of the latter, but has left the former rather more keen to farm these high risk services out.

Following a reorganization of local government, a director of social work for one of the large childcare charities visited the new authority to introduce himself. He was at pains to impress on his hosts that he was not seeking new work as the current workload was straining his current resources. Despite this, he left with three new projects and yet more in the future. The task is not marketing services to needy local authorities but marketing that relationship to the public at large.

There are significant differences between the marketing strategies used to raise profile, awareness and funds and those used in marketing services. For the statutory sector, it is crucial for the agency to have the appropriate services available where and when they are needed. There is a need to demonstrate that these services are safe, supported by best practice, quality assurance, staff training programmes and complaint processes.

The range of statutory bodies involved is huge. For example, a childcare charity offering comprehensive care and support services will need to negotiate with any or all of the following, far from exhaustive, list:

■ the social services;
■ education authorities;
■ the probation service;
■ youth justice;
■ health authorities;
■ the police;
■ The Health and Safety Executive;
■ family mediation services;
■ local housing authorities;
■ town planning.

Thus, it can be seen that individual charities need to possess a wide range of operational experience and policy expertise. These require marketing. No agency, to my knowledge, has yet addressed the potential time bomb here. Why should the public fund a supposedly voluntary agency, the greater majority of whose work is the provision of statutory services? Are they thereby funding the work of the Exchequer? The public perception of charities will be much altered by the debate. There is a formidable marketing task here, and, reading between the lines, one on which the UK government has already embarked.

Charities are going to need to emphasize that the added value of their quality assured services is not funded by the statutory agreements. Despite many care orientated charities receiving the greater bulk of their funding through the provision of services, that added value persuades local authorities. Hence the need for continuing voluntary funding.

Marketing of services to fulfil current need is not the work of a marketing specialist, but of a qualified care professional with marketing skills. However, those skills will be stretched when attempting to market innovation without the requirements of statutory obligation. One thinks of community-based initiatives like credit unions, self-help projects, alternatives to custody schemes, mediation and conciliation services among many. The adoption of such ideas will require a marketing strategy aimed at local authorities, central government policy makers and the public at large. It will probably drive currently competing charities into greater cooperation and bring greater clarity to fundraising objectives.

Part 2

Who are our customers?

This section looks at the different markets in which charities operate.

3

Marketing to donors

Paula Keaveney

Charities get their income from a range of sources. These include fees and grants from government or other governmental sources, fees from individuals, income from investments and income from the sale of property or land. The other major source of money is a mix referred to as voluntary income. This can be money from a trust, a company or from an individual or group. It can be a one-off donation or a regular gift. The giver can consciously decide to support a cause (for example, by responding to a specific appeal) or have no interest in the cause getting the money (for example, by buying a raffle ticket for the prize). The money can be seen purely as a gift or as an investment that will bring a return (many company donations or sponsorship deals are made in the commercial interests of the company).

Motivations are different, sizes of donation are different, interests are different and rewards are different. This chapter is about the 'donor market'. It is immediately obvious that there are not one but many donor markets, and some of these will not view themselves as donors. Not only is there a wide range of different markets but also a wide range of fundraising marketing techniques. A glimpse through the job advertisements placed by any large charity will show at once the range of specialisms that have developed.

For a small charity, this can seem extremely daunting. Yet it need not, for what matters is not detailed knowledge of the techniques, but an understanding of the relevant markets and of how to meet their needs and demands in a way that brings in money for the charity. No amount of technique will help if the market is not understood properly.

> A major national charity had an extensive network of volunteer groups. These groups of (mainly) middle-aged and elderly ladies met regularly, organizing social events that raised considerable sums of money. Most of the work was done by word of mouth. The volunteers enjoyed the involvement and the social contact. As part of an effort to ensure no fundraising opportunity was missed, the names and addresses of the volunteers were added to a database used to send out a direct mail shot about legacies. The volunteers were horrified and took up every opportunity to tell the staff so.
>
> They were not objecting to the suggestion of the will making – many had in fact already thought of this. They were not objecting to an attempt to keep them informed of other fundraising developments within the charity – many were very interested in the accounts given by staff visiting their meetings. What had annoyed the volunteers was the type of communication used.
>
> They were used to relating to the charity through personal, face-to-face communication. They had chosen to be volunteers and enjoyed the special status this appeared to give. Yet, with one push of a button, a direct mail shot had moved them from special individual to one of an impersonal mailing list. In this case, not enough attention was paid to the nature of the market.

The donor market can be divided and then subdivided in several ways. A commonly used division is between individuals and organizations.

WAYS ORGANIZATIONS SUPPORT CHARITIES

■ Charitable trusts – give grants for specific things.
■ Companies – can support charities in a range of ways, through sponsorship, one-off donations or gifts in kind.
■ Clubs and societies – can give donations, organize events and provide opportunities to generate interest from their members.

WAYS INDIVIDUALS SUPPORT CHARITIES

■ donations;
■ legacies;
■ volunteering;
■ buying raffle tickets;
■ sponsoring people or being sponsored.

A less obvious, but important, distinction is between deliberate and accidental givers. Much basic charity fundraising actually targets accidental givers. By using this term, I do not mean that they are unaware they have handed over money – merely that they do not know, or are not particularly concerned about, the charity to which the money goes. Often the motivation for giving does not come from the particular cause. Examples are: raffles, where the motivation is the prize; quizzes and other games, where the motivation is the fun and the prize; jumble sales, boot sales and other trading, where the motivation is the cheap goods. Accidental giving is also a feature of larger charities. How many people, for example, would be 'brand loyal' to their local charity shop? They might shop there because they like the staff, or the window display or its convenience for the bus stop – but usually not for the name. Accidental donors, however, do need to be understood in the same way as deliberate givers.

There is nothing wrong with accidental donors. But, by their very nature, accidental donors will never turn into regular supporters of the charity. And it is only through developing regular support that a charity can gain the confidence and stability it needs in its finances. For small and medium-sized charities it is well worth spending some time analysing how much of the money raised from individuals can be classed as 'accidental'. If this is a high proportion, and a high proportion of staff or senior volunteer time goes into raising it, the charity could have a problem. If not enough time or effort can be spent on developing deliberate support then it will become ever harder to identify new markets.

However, developing deliberate donors is easier said than done. Many chapters in this book touch on techniques and approaches that can be used. For most charities, this will be a case of starting with existing supporters. Even if not currently defined as donors, all charities will have a group of people who can be identified as supporters. The task is to help the supporters develop into donors, members and advocates of the charity. The chapter on relationship marketing throws helpful light on this issue.

Charity marketers, like marketers in other sectors, have become ever more focused on the individual and on specific market segments. Direct mail, in particular, can be very cleverly targeted. Yet, there is evidence that significant numbers of people prefer face-to-face or human contact of some sort. The 1990s, for example, saw the development of a form of street fundraising that involves stopping people on the high street.

The fact that some donor markets prefer one form of communication to another is a vital issue to understand. Research into the demographics of charity support, in particular by Judith Nichols, who is a US-based fundraising consultant, has shown that different groups will behave very differently in their relationships with charities. Whereas some age groups will view charity giving as a duty, others will want to get something back, whether it be a sense of feeling good or a pack of membership information. Charities wanting to do more thinking about different donor markets and their attitudes would be well advised to spend time looking at the existing research (some of the organizations listed in Appendix 2 of this book can help).

A good example of technique taking over from knowledge of the market is the development of fundraising via the Internet. It is possible to fundraise via the World Wide Web and there are a number of books on the subject. A Web site that leads with fundraising messages, however, will fail because it shows a basic misunderstanding of the market (of Net users) and the medium. An individual logging on to a Web site about a medical condition is usually someone with the condition and seeking information (which might be a matter of life or death for him or her), a professional wanting to know how to work with a particular client, or a student doing research. None of this group will want the first few pages to be requests for money. Where this happens, their need is not met and they may simply find another site. If, however, your site focuses mainly on your cause, or on the vital information people need, you may be able to keep your visitors for longer, and encourage repeat visits. This is when a visitor may look further and feel motivated to give. (Web sites are tackled in Chapter 5.)

Understanding the donor markets, and the ways in which they like to relate to the charity, is vital for charities. It is also vital to be aware of trends within any of the markets. In the 'accidental' market, for example, there are clear trends in UK retailing that are seeing charity-shop profitability being affected by the growth of discount clothes stores. This sort of information is key to decisions charities might make about expanding their shops' operation.

In the deliberate markets, experts say that increasing attention to donor opinions and needs is crucial. According to Judith Nichols:

> We need to become less driven by methodology and more by our donors – worrying less about annual appeals, special events, capital campaigns and listening more to how and when donors want to give.
>
> Nichols, J (2000) *Third Sector*, 19 October

4

Marketing to opinion formers – political communications in the voluntary sector

David Hughes

A common task facing virtually all organizations in the voluntary sector is that of bringing effective influence to bear on government and on those who help shape its decisions. Whether seeking primary legislation, regulatory change or additional public funds, voluntary organizations need to be effective in the field of political communication if they are to achieve what many of their members and supporters see as their primary goals.

However, activity in this area – now generally encompassed in the catch-all phrase 'lobbying' – developed in recent years from a little-known and misunderstood activity to a controversial but still misunderstood one. This situation raises particular issues for the voluntary sector.

The first of these is the scepticism that many employees and activists in the voluntary sector feel towards lobbying. The suspect behaviour in recent years of both some parliamentarians and some lobbyists has produced a perception that such activities are dependent on large financial resources, the exploitation of personal contacts and on other practices that distort the democratic process. Although the high profile controversies that have taken place have involved companies and individuals in the commercial sector, some key figures in voluntary organizations may not wish to run the risk of seeing their organizations 'tainted' through involvement in this field, or may be reluctant to commit the staff resources and members' contributions required to carry out such work effectively.

Nonetheless, in many cases activity in this field is vital to the realization of the organization's objectives. Whether a voluntary organization is active in the field of the environment, disability, poverty, overseas development, conservation, animal welfare or any other major concern, the degree of its success will probably rest in the hands of at least one, if not several, government departments. Consequently, political communications should not merely be tolerated behind the scenes, but must be accepted as playing a central role in an organization's work. At the same time, however, voluntary organizations must approach lobbying with a style and philosophy that ensure that they are not vulnerable to the criticisms attracted by some commercial practitioners in recent years.

Furthermore, voluntary organizations enjoy several advantages over commercial interests when it comes to lobbying. The most important of these is the fact that virtually all the organization's lobbying targets will be willing to recognize its benevolent motivation and intent, even if they do not agree with its particular point of view. Few politicians will want to be seen to be attacking a charity with a degree of popular support in the way they might criticize a major company or trade association. Although there are exceptions – Greenpeace or the League Against Cruel Sports, for example – representatives of most charities and voluntary organizations will be respected at face value by the vast majority of their target audiences.

THE BUILDING BLOCKS OF EFFECTIVE LOBBYING – DEFINING THE ORGANIZATION'S CASE

An effective lobbying campaign demands considerable advance internal planning before any external audiences are engaged.

First, the campaign's key objectives should be clarified and prioritized, complete with a recognition that some objectives might have to be sacrificed for the achievement of others, and an understanding of what is the organization's 'bottom line' beyond which compromise is not acceptable.

Secondly, the particulars of the case should be set out in a concise and factual way, highlighting the points which are most likely to resonate with the campaign's key targets. This process should include a recognition and rebuttal of countervailing points and other weaknesses. This is often best achieved by carrying out a SWOT (Strengths, Weaknesses, Opportunities and Threats) analysis, which will help you both brief a wider internal group on your case and identify some of the strategic issues you face. No matter how much 'justice is on your side', it is important to acknowledge that virtually all of your target audiences will have less interest in your case than your own staff and supporters. For this reason you must face the discipline of distilling the case down to a brief, tightly written document, capable of being summarized in just a couple of sides of A4.

The process will produce much internal anguish, with colleagues pressing hard for the additional inclusion of one more scientific fact, or one more case history, to which they attach a particular importance. Each addition, however, will in fact reduce the likelihood of the case being read at all. This does not mean that such additional material cannot subsequently be made available to a keen third-party advocate or a key target whose interest has been aroused. Even then, however, the sympathetic politician with dozens of issues on his or her agenda should not be swamped with extraneous detail.

What the organization should do is identify a few key messages related to the heart of the argument, which should be repeated by every spokesperson, in every piece of literature or communication, and at every meeting with a key contact or target. Even when expressed in emotional terms, these key messages must nonetheless be firmly rooted in fact and easily understood by the layperson.

THE BUILDING BLOCKS OF EFFECTIVE LOBBYING... IDENTIFYING THE ORGANIZATION'S TARGETS

At the heart of your campaign must be the creation of a series of opportunities to communicate your key messages and case, preferably in person, but sometimes only in writing, to a wide range of key targets.

You must therefore correctly identify not only the key decision makers, but also the wider group of individuals who will influence them. Also, it is vital that you understand each target's real level of power in the political process. This is a consideration that is often separate from an individual's formal status or position. You must also recognize that the decision you are hoping to influence may well rest in the hands of just a single minister, and you will be lucky if you meet that individual just once during the course of your campaign.

However, a minister's decision will almost certainly be influenced by dozens if not hundreds of other individuals, many of whom will certainly be much more accessible. Some of these influencers can be easily identified through the formal position they hold – a minister's special adviser, a parliamentary private sectary (PPS), the civil servant handling the issue and the relevant member of the No 10 Policy Unit for instance. Special advisers and PPSs are particularly useful as they can often be used to short circuit the formal Whitehall process and bring key issues to the minister's attention more rapidly. In addition, they will generally be more sensitive to the political nuances and opportunities of a particular issue if you can make the case that the actions you are seeking can produce a political benefit for either the minister or the government. Members of the No 10 Policy Unit can play a similar role, and can initiate interest in an issue in Downing Street – particularly useful if the minister or department is being slow, uninterested or hostile.

In looking at others one step removed from the formal process of government, it is important to have a clear understanding of the real role and influence of backbench MPs. Unlike legislators in the USA, for example, MPs hardly ever affect political outcomes through the casting of their individual votes. The discipline of the

British party system and the prevalence of secure government majorities mean that the lobbyist is rarely engaged in the process of 'counting heads' for or against a particular item of legislation. Although conscience issues such as Sunday trading, abortion and animal welfare provide occasional exceptions, the lobbyist should usually be seeking a parliamentarian's support in less dramatic fashion. This might take the form of joining a delegation to the minister, or through various parliamentary tactics such as the signing of an Early Day Motion, the asking of a question or the holding of an adjournment or 10-minute-rule bill debate.

MPs who are officers or members of relevant select or backbench committees and all-party groups should also be reviewed as potential allies. Some might have developed a reputation for expertise in your own given area, or might be sufficiently senior to be consulted by ministers from time to time. It might also be worth persuading select committee members to hold an inquiry into the issues with which your campaign is concerned.

However, asking an individual or group of MPs to vote against a central piece of the government's legislative programme is in reality an admission of defeat and is likely to be rebuffed. A successful campaign will have changed government thinking at a much earlier stage of the legislative process – trying to promote a last-minute rebellion is little more than a gesture and is likely to produce ongoing bad feeling between the voluntary organization and the government.

Ironically, the position of members of the House of Lords is subtly different. Although the subordinate chamber, party discipline is also weaker. Since reform of the House, no government is likely to have a majority and for most Peers considerations of personal advancement or ambition are ancient history! Peers also have a strong respect for experts in particular fields and votes can therefore be swayed. Procedures such as the unstarred question also allow an issue to be well aired at 'peak time'. Sympathetic Peers who are expert in your field are valuable allies with whom close ongoing contact should be maintained.

Furthermore, recent constitutional changes have widened the range of potential influencers to include members of the devolved assemblies in Scotland, Wales, Northern Ireland and London, and the members of the Regional Development Agencies and their consultative 'chambers'. The powers of these bodies vary enormously: from minimal to those of the Scottish Parliament, which is free to legislate in a number of areas at variance with Westminster. Moreover, none of these bodies is dominated by a single party and many of their members will be looking for opportunities to make an impact on behalf of both themselves and the body in question. Issues pushed to the fore in one of these bodies will inevitably produce some response from central government, and will provide opportunities for the wider publicizing of an issue.

It is also worth focusing on party personnel who are either responsible for relevant policy areas or who are known to be influential with relevant ministers or shadow spokespeople. Similarly, think tanks are useful as both sources of influence and worthwhile filters to provide a practicality 'health check' for your proposals.

Consideration should also be given to whether the institutions of the EU are relevant to your campaign. If so, MEPs, commission officials and officials at the UK's permanent representation should feature in your campaign, as should the identification of allies and supporters from other EU countries.

It is also important, when compiling lists of targets, to identify and evaluate your existing relationships and links with the individuals in question. You should therefore undertake a 'political contact audit' of all your officers, staff and activists to identify which relationships are already in place and the extent to which they can be harnessed and then deployed as part of your new campaign. Clearly, a legislator with interest in, or familiarity with, your work is far more likely to be supportive than one you are approaching for the first time. This does not mean that you should rely totally on such existing contacts and neglect the need to form new links with other key individuals. Nor should you shirk an honest appraisal of how such figures are viewed by their colleagues. Sometimes an advocate for a particular issue will be taken less seriously precisely because he is so associated with it. The audit process will also minimize the risk of freelance activity by members of your organization of which you are unaware, and which might lead to confusion in terms of either actions or messages.

THE BUILDING BLOCKS OF EFFECTIVE LOBBYING... TIMING AND PROCESS

It is important to develop a proper understanding of both the timing and process relating to the decision you seek to influence. This will depend partly on whether you are seeking to initiate fresh government action, or whether you are aiming to shape the outcome of a process already set in train. Either way you will need to work out the process the government will go through and when it will reach its conclusion. Trying to alter a decision once it has been made and publicly announced is much more difficult than shaping policy as it is formed. The civil servants with the brief covering your area of concern are a vital source of information in this regard. Even if they are not wholly sympathetic to your view, they are unlikely to conceal the nature of the processes and the timetable from you. However, it is also vital that your input is positive and provides practical solutions to the issue in question. A simple restatement of opposition will probably lead to your exclusion from the ongoing debate.

Additionally, you will need to set up an effective monitoring and political intelligence gathering capability. This should ensure that you are fully aware of all developments in Westminster and Whitehall affecting your agenda and of what they mean. Selective information from such a service should be circulated not only to your immediate campaign team, but also to other key personnel to keep them informed. Such a service is best provided by one of the specialist firms in the field that can meet prompt deadlines and work to a precise brief. The raw information should, however, be supported by a specific analysis of its implications, which might be best written by a consultant or expert member of staff.

A final point is to ensure that your campaign is not likely to fall foul of the laws on charities and politics. It will be important to be even-handed across the political parties, to check that your document and arguments are factually based and to make sure that what you are doing relates to the core objectives of your organization.

Before you start, make sure you are fully aware of your assets (including knowledge, reputation and staff) and make sure that your campaign plan uses these to your advantage.

EFFECTIVE LOBBYING

It is vital that as well as highlighting the shortcomings of the existing situation, you are able to provide workable solutions. There is no point in simply criticizing without providing an alternative. The more you make it easy for the government to choose your option, the more likely you are to succeed.

This process entails working with government rather than continuously adopting a stance of outright opposition. Although there may be times when you will need to highlight your disagreements, be sure to maintain a constructive dialogue at the same time, and do not descend to personal attacks on ministers or officials.

Try to demonstrate that there is a strong body of public support for your stance. However worthwhile your cause, you will be more likely to be successful if politicians believe there is a political benefit in supporting you. These factors will also determine the extent to which they will make your cause a personal priority commanding their ongoing attention. Many politicians have fixed ideas about what matters to the public. Try to correct this if necessary, either by conducting opinion polling among the general public or party activists or floating voters, or by attempting to secure substantial media coverage that will also reinforce the salience of the issue in the minds of your targets. A politician who has heard about your issue on the *Today Programme*, or read about it in the morning paper, will be much more likely to read your brief at the office a few hours later. On this point, it is worth remembering that newspapers like the London *Evening Standard* have an influence beyond their natural boundaries, as MPs and their staff will read this newspaper during their week in London.

To this end, it will be useful to assemble a range of independent third parties who will be prepared to endorse your position publicly, and perhaps act as ongoing advocates. These might include academics with a relevant track record, influential think tanks, popular opinion formers and media personalities.

All meetings with key targets should be carefully choreographed in advance. Before the meeting, find out who will be there and what amount of time you have. Confirm who will speak on your side, what they will say and who will respond to which questions. Do not take a large delegation, even if internal diplomacy seems to demand it. Everyone present should have a purpose. Provide follow-up material and take agreed actions speedily.

INTEGRATED CAMPAIGNING

In the past some government relations practitioners argued that their activities should take place in a vacuum, isolated from other communications activities. Although this can occasionally be the case, when dealing with civil servants over a highly technical or scientific point for instance, it is generally untrue, and ignores the realities of the importance politicians attach to the wider media agenda.

A key feature of most successful lobbying campaigns today is the successful integration of political communications with other activities. As mentioned above, it is always important for politicians to be convinced that an issue has wide public support and that favourable campaign action will therefore produce a political dividend. Deployment of a wide range of campaigning techniques will help both demonstrate public support and mobilize it, while lobbying activity that is undertaken in isolation is not likely to lead to politicians prioritizing the issue.

Lobbying should therefore be part of a mix that might include media relations, advertising, targeted mail shots, opinion polling and public meetings. A particularly successful example of this type of integrated approach were the campaigns undertaken some years ago by the Royal Society for the Prevention of Cruelty to Animals (RSPCA) concerning issues like the transport of live animals for export and those of dangerous dogs. Intensely political campaigns were backed up by high profile advertising and direct mail, each of which won more converts to the issue who were then encouraged to communicate their views to their MPs. The media attention generated also served to persuade many politicians that the issues commanded a greater salience with the public than they had previously imagined. This view was reinforced by opinion polling activity. What is more, successful, issue specific fundraising undertaken during the campaign more than covered the considerable financial outlay of this approach. The RSPCA's staff harnessed a range of specialist agencies that both fulfilled particular needs and liaised with one another to maximum effect.

The result was both a high public profile for the campaigns and movement on the part of the politicians, who had come to believe that they could no longer ignore what they saw as a mounting tide of public concern.

Today, such integrated campaigns should also make full use of the Internet and e-mail, tools that enable speedy communication with supporters who can be updated on key developments and encouraged to express their concerns to legislators immediately. All the political parties, government departments, local authorities and many individual legislators can now be contacted by e-mail, and most take any surge of opinion coming through these media particularly seriously.

INEFFECTIVE CAMPAIGNING... OR WHAT NOT TO DO

As lobbying has grown, so has the number of legends surrounding it as well as a number of undesirable and ineffective practices. You should never offer to make any form of payment or provide any other form of reward to any legislator or official who you are trying to influence. Not only is this a waste and an abuse of your resources, it is likely to create a negative image among people you are trying to win over.

Do not entertain without a purpose. The only politicians likely to be willing to while away several hours having lunch are not likely to be very influential. You are far more likely to get results from the target who can only spare 20 minutes over a cup of tea. Plan exactly what you will say, what actions you wish the target to take and undertake follow-up promptly.

Do not let your plan be derailed by a well-meaning colleague or supporter who believes that he – and it always is a he – can provide miraculous results through the 'old boy network'. Although such sources can sometimes facilitate access, they are unlikely to change government policy over a glass of port at the Athenaeum!

Do not undertake vast, impersonal mass mailings of the entire membership of the House of Commons. Material like this goes straight in the bin, and can irritate the supporter who sees himself or herself treated in the same way as all the other MPs. Do not encourage your supporters to inundate MPs with identical post-cards or letters with no personal input.

Do not take it as read that civil servants will have as great a knowledge of the issue as you do. Most officials are generalists by background and will probably be covering a broader range of issues than those in which you have a direct interest. They will therefore appreciate a source of fresh expertise and will welcome being able to develop an ongoing relationship with you even if they do not always agree with you. Such a relationship may well also serve to give you advance warning of other key developments.

Do not overload your targets with superfluous information unless they ask for it, and recognize when a target has been won over. You must be consistent in your key message and accurate in any information you provide, whether to a supporter whom you hope will use it on your behalf, or an opponent who might attack you. Always make it clear when you are passing on opinion as opposed to fact.

Finally, do not lose a sense of perspective, including an understanding of your targets' agendas and priorities. A lobbyist for an out-of-town supermarket development once objected to the postponement of a meeting with an MP on the day that 3,000 of his constituents were made redundant.

DO YOU NEED A CONSULTANT?

Even more controversial than lobbying itself are the professional companies working in the field. A voluntary organization with a reputation and charitable status to protect needs to think carefully about how to use consultancy expertise.

The key to a relationship is to make sure that the consultancy does not supplant the client as the voice and presence of the campaign. Consultancies can make a range of contributions as sources of expert advice about the political process, about the cultures and agendas of government departments and about the individual political parties. They can also be a source of objective opinion about your case and the progress you are making. However, consultants should not play the role of paid advocates, supplanting your own spokespeople. Most politicians will want to meet and speak with the actual organization and its representatives, and are likely to form a lower opinion of any organization that chooses to abdicate from this role.

Similarly, the commercial relationship with paid consultants should be defined at an early stage, with an emphasis on the ongoing availability of expert and/or senior staff, the need to avoid conflicts of interest, the ethical stance of the consultancy and the relevant financial arrangements. Broadly speaking, the voluntary organization will get better value for money if the relationship is based on payment for work done in achieving specific goals and targets rather than on the payment of an open-ended retainer.

CONCLUSION

Effective lobbying depends on making a factual case in an honest way to the right people at the right time while demonstrating both public support and a concern for the public interest.

In doing this, an organization needs to deploy a case which can withstand the intellectual scrutiny of the civil service and which takes account of wider political realities and interests.

During the course of your campaign, you should be constantly evaluating your effectiveness – generally by reference to third parties – and adapting to the developing situation. You should be ready to be flexible while not losing sight of your bottom-line objectives. You should know when to accept as good an outcome as you are going to get.

Keep ownership and control of your campaign. Take advice from consultants but remain your own advocates. Finally, aim to form friendly, long-term relationships with your targets and those around them – it should make success easier next time.

Part 3

Tools and techniques

5

Marketing on the Internet

Paula Keaveney and Mike Ward

Recent years have seen a marked growth in the use of the Internet by charities. Many large organizations now have specific staff posts for Web site or 'new media' editors. Others have set up basic sites replicating parts of their annual report. Debate has moved on to whether or not significant fundraising can be achieved via the Net.

This chapter is not about how to set up a Web site. Neither is it about the rash of affinity schemes now linked to Web access and pioneered by charities like Oxfam and umbrella organizations like Care 4 Free. This chapter is about the use of the Internet and new media more generally in a charity's marketing plans. (References to other resources on Web sites and the Internet are included in Appendix 1 in this book.)

FIRST, ASK 'WHY?'

The first task for any charity, of whatever size, is to consider carefully why exactly it wants a Web site. Many sites appear to have been set up because 'we ought to have one' or 'every other charity has one'. This is not enough of an adequate rationale for creating a site. Creation of a site can be relatively simple. Maintenance and updating, however, can call for resources that do not exist in-house – with the result that the site becomes less accurate and less attractive. An inaccurate, outdated Web site that does not provide quick response to contacts can do positive harm to your image. So it is vital to think about the 'why', define marketing and communications objectives, and analyse your own capacity before taking any further steps.

There are several basic principles to bear in mind when thinking about using the Web as part of charity marketing. Lack of thought about these will certainly cause problems later on:

1. Understand the nature of the medium and what users therefore expect. There are clear implications for writing, design, maintenance and staffing in the nature of the World Wide Web.
2. Understand how your readers are likely to navigate around the Web. Again, there are clear implications for writing and presentation in the unique way readers navigate.
3. Understand how your Web site will fit into your overall communications.

THE NATURE OF THE MEDIUM AND WHAT THAT MEANS FOR CHARITIES

On one level, the World Wide Web is the ultimate personalized form of communication. Unlike a mail shot, each person can get exactly the right information for himself or herself, picking and choosing from a Web site and skipping over anything not relevant. The Web is also, however, an ultimate form of mass communication. It is like a billboard that, in theory, anyone in the world can see.

The Internet also encourages response. Users of the Net expect to be able to send messages by e-mail directly to Web sites. They expect to be able to ask questions, give comments, buy products, sign petitions and so on.

It is vital to understand how these two factors could cause problems for a charity that has not planned properly.

DEALING WITH RESPONSES

Anyone involved in marketing a charity will work hard to select the right markets for its services, its fundraising messages or its campaigns. This is a basic principle of marketing. A Web site, however, is there for anybody, whoever he or she is and wherever he or she lives. This begins to matter when users are encouraged to ask questions. Given that the World Wide Web is international, unless your target market is literally the world, there is a strong possibility that a charity will receive more comments from outside its target market than from within it. A UK medical research charity, for example, found that less than 20 per cent of the people viewing its Web site were from the United Kingdom. If, however, this had resulted in a barrage of time-consuming questions from outside the United Kingdom, that charity would have faced a problem, as no clear policy existed on which questions to prioritize.

So any planning needs to bear the international dimension in mind. If your charity has partner organizations around the world, it is worth agreeing a protocol so that questions from 'off your patch' are forwarded to the partner for a reply. You also need to think carefully about how you are going to phrase any offers to mail out paperwork on request.

Even if a Web site does not yield responses from outside the target market, the need to reply to e-mails can still cause significant problems. The electronic nature of the medium has an effect on the psychology of the communication. Whereas someone sending a letter will expect a few days of delay before a reply is received, time scales with e-mail are shorter. If the charity is not able to check messages at least daily, and provide a proper system for speedy replies, it needs to think carefully about whether it is ready for a Web site. The problem, of course, is that the e-mail contents and their replies may be tangential to the charity's marketing plan and mission. In this case, the charity becomes driven by the medium in a way that fails to meet marketing objectives. To minimize this, it is worth thinking about ways of defining question areas. To cut down repetitive work, it is well worth thinking about the 20 most likely questions and posting them and the answers on a 'frequently asked questions' page. As other questions become frequent, they can be added.

HOW READERS BEHAVE AND WHAT THIS IS LIKELY TO MEAN

Questioning, not browsing

Because the World Wide Web offers so much choice for users, it is important to design your site in a way that meets their needs. Someone looking at the National Society for the Prevention of Cruelty to Children (NSPCC) Web site, for example, may not be looking for the NSPCC *per se*, but for material about children. His or her search engine has provided the NSPCC address along with a host of others. Most Web site users will not be looking for information about the charity, but for information about the subjects you cover. This is a vital point to take on board as the vast majority of charity Web sites treat the reader as someone who is already interested in, and in fact very familiar with, the internal structure of that charity. To understand this, think of the way in which phone callers without knowledge of departmental divisions in large organizations are often misdirected by switchboards.

The most common way for a charity new to Web sites to create one is to ask each department to provide something for a page. The reader is then often left to guess what is on each page from a department title that is far from clear. To understand this, think about the different department titles in charities that do similar things, or those titles that could in fact mean anything. What are 'support services' for example – IT, admin, donation receipts or information and advice? Even if the department name is clear, the activities of that department may still be expressed in a way of no relevance to the reader. Authors of Web sites, and to a certain extent authors of annual reports, need to understand above everything else that very few people care about which section of the charity performs a service; they want to know what the service is.

Before structuring, writing and designing a Web site, a charity should put itself in the position of potential users. A disability charity may consider that users are likely to include:

▧ parents and carers with disabled children;
▧ social workers and other professionals;
▧ students doing research projects;
▧ members and existing supporters of the charity.

It might then identify the needs of the parents group as wanting:

▓ to find out if there are services a family can use;
▓ basic information about ways they can help their child;
▓ to know about their rights re education and other statutory provision.

If you carry out this exercise for each main market or group, you can structure your Web site to meet the needs of the markets you particularly want to meet. This will almost definitely mean writing copy that crosses departmental responsibilities.

It will be immediately obvious that if this approach is to be taken, the Web site author must not hand over responsibility for writing sections to individual departments but should start from the viewpoint of each likely market and collect the information and contacts relevant to each.

LOST IN SPACE?

Most people start a book or a magazine by looking at the front page. If we come into a TV programme half way through, we can at least refer to a newspaper or magazine to find out what it is. Yet, it is quite possible to arrive at a page in a Web site without really knowing where you are and without seeing any context.

The World Wide Web thrives on such connectivity. It is possible to link from a page in one organization's Web site to a page half way through a completely different organization's site. Depending on how the page is designed and written, this can cause considerable confusion.

It is vital to bear these navigation possibilities in mind when sites are designed and when pages are written. Whereas in a magazine we can treat a three-page article as one story, each Web site screen needs to be seen as one story exploring a different angle or theme.

Achieving this will depend on the way you are designing and writing, but it is vital to ensure some element of context on each single screen. A simple example of how this is done can be seen on TV on teletext. Careful reading of each screen will show phrases setting a story in context so that the reader can understand what is going on whichever screen he or she comes across first. You may also decide to add context by including a common header or footer heading on each screen, or a short explanatory phrase and navigation bar with logo as a common feature at the side.

SCREEN ONLY?

If one of your objectives is to communicate complex information usually presented as fact sheets, it is vital that your pages are presented in a way in which the information can be easily printed off. Users may also need to print off donation forms, petitions and so on. For example, think very carefully before designing pages with strong colours in the background. If users try to print from your site and fail, they are likely to look elsewhere for information in the future.

FITTING INTO OVERALL COMMUNICATIONS OBJECTIVES

If your charity is thinking properly about marketing and communications, it will have established clear messages to communicate about itself. It will have a clear idea of whom it is trying to reach. This will be carried through a range of materials and activities, from the annual review to fundraising mail shots.

Ironically however, when it comes to the communication with the biggest audience potential – the Web site users – charities often forget to include this in their thinking, choosing to ask someone to come up with a Web site as an add on.

For a Web site to play its role in supporting and reinforcing overall messages, it is vital that it is incorporated fully into the communications plan. This is a strong argument for editorial responsibility for the Web site lying with a head of marketing or head of communications. In small charities, it means the same person must oversee both the Web site and all the printed materials.

EFFECTIVE USE OF WEB SITES

For any advertising message to get across, a certain amount of repetition is needed. Not only do you want your messages to reinforce one another across all your communications, you need your Web site to achieve some repetition through repeat visits by users. This is particularly important if you want to raise funds through your Web site. The chance of a first-time visitor making a donation is very slim.

There are a number of ways of encouraging repeat visits. 'Latest news' pages or 'research update' pages, if updated regularly enough, will prompt interested people to bookmark your page and come back repeatedly. A developing 'Frequently Asked Questions' section or a 'Guest book' will also provide extra value.

Membership or special interest pages, with passwords or addresses given only to certain groups, can be used for bulletin boards or discussion groups that, by being seen as special, encourage regular visits. Many professional organizations' Web sites include a 'public' section and a 'members' section.

EFFECTIVE USE OF E-MAIL

Many charities are now beginning to use e-mail as a way of keeping their supporters informed and updated. Even if you are not yet ready to do this, it is well worth starting now to collect e-mail addresses of supporters whenever you can. There are some communications, particularly for groups that have registered a special interest or have joined a scheme, which are ideal for e-mailing. News of a breakthrough in medical research, or advance news of a broadcast about the charity, are two examples of when e-mailing supporters would work well.

It is important, however, to establish a corporate style for these group e-mails, and to beware that the informality and speed of e-mails can cause you to become overly chatty. News can be urgent and formal at the same time, and it is vital not to lose the importance of what you are trying to say through a bad choice of tone and style.

RESEARCHING WEB SITES

Before embarking on a new Web site, or making changes to your existing site, it is well worth looking at a range of other sites run by similar charities, or similar sized organizations. Look at each site and ask yourself what that charity is trying to achieve. Test how easy it is to find your way around. Try printing off pages if appropriate. Check the guest book or frequently asked questions pages. If colour images are used, see how long it takes the picture to appear fully on your screen. (Before your own site goes live, you will need to carry out these and other tasks, to check your Web site.)

QUESTIONS TO ASK BEFORE SETTING UP A WEB SITE

■ Why do we need a Web site?
■ Do we have the resources to update and to respond?
■ Who is going to take overall responsibility?
■ Should we create in-house or use a freelancer?
■ How will we encourage repeat visits?
■ How will we monitor who is using the site?
■ Do we want people to print off our material?
■ Which other sites should we link to?

Key words in new media

It is worth being familiar with some of the terms used, particularly if you are about to meet a Web site consultant:

■ FAQ – Frequently Asked Questions.
■ Guest book – a section of the Web site allowing people to sign in by posting messages. These can be public, seen by all visitors to the site, or private, and seen by the Web site editors only. Guest books help people ask and answer their own questions. They can be abused and need checking on a regular basis.

- Bookmark – Internet users can bookmark their favourite sites. By clicking on an icon on their screen, they add the address of the site to a list that their computer then keeps. This means they can return to the site again without typing in the address.
- URL – Uniform Resource Locator – another word for the address of the page in the site. Each site has an address, with each section in the site having a longer address. A box, usually at the top of the screen, contains this address.
- Search engine – this searches the Web for a subject or keyword and provides lists of sites matching the word. The sites will be those 'tagged' with the keyword. When creating a site, it is important to make full use of the tags to attract more visitors.
- www = World Wide Web. This is not the same as the Internet. The Web is the interface that allows text, data and multimedia to be offered and accessed globally on the Internet. The Internet is the infrastructure that also carries other traffic such as e-mail.
- 'Surfing the Net' – looking through what is available. This is a bit like flicking through an encyclopaedia assembled at random.
- Password – a word or combination of letters and/or numbers that allows access to all or part of a site. This is often used for access to the members' section of a Web site.
- Navigation bar or buttons – part of the screen often looking like a column or series of buttons that allows the user to move to another part of the Web site.
- Home Page – the base page of the site. A little like the combined title, contents and introduction in a book. Many users will start with this page. It is important to allow users to return to the home page at any point and to include a contents list or introductory explanation on this page.

6

Relationship marketing and membership schemes

Susan Kay-Williams

INTRODUCTION

Whilst the title may give the impression that these two areas are intrinsically linked, and indeed, forward looking membership schemes should be run on relationship marketing principles, the two topics are different enough to be examined separately.

The first part of this chapter examines the principles of relationship marketing and how to apply them to non-profit organizations. The second part looks at membership schemes, focusing particularly on why, when and how to establish one.

RELATIONSHIP MARKETING

The term 'relationship marketing' came, like most marketing terms, from the commercial sector, where it has been seen as a development of direct marketing. This mindset arose because early practitioners linked relationship marketing techniques to the rise of computer technology, which made direct access to and interrogation of data much easier.

However, true relationship marketing demands a lot more than just a good database. It is a philosophy requiring a strategic approach, not simply a set of techniques. It is about adopting an attitude that puts the person, the customer or supporter, before his or her purchase or donation. It is about looking at supporters as individuals, not reference numbers, and it is about building long-term relationships rather than just securing the one-off donation, however large.

This more strategic and proactive view of customers as people is most famously expounded in Peppers and Rogers' work (1993). They propose that the only way forward for business is to jettison the concepts of mass marketing and build customer relationships one person at a time.

To the average charity manager, this might sound a little too slow to meet his or her need for income. Burnett takes a more realistic approach for charities in his groundbreaking book *Relationship Fundraising* (1992), though he was at pains not to call this marketing.

During the late 1990s, the impact of such books, combined with the increase in commercial marketing people entering the charity sector and the widespread 'upskilling' of professional fundraisers, have enabled charities to take a strategic view of their activities. As a result, relationship marketing is finding its niche within the non-profit sector.

In fact, the special characteristics of non-profit organizations mean that we can often apply relationship marketing more holistically than commercial companies. I was once invited to speak at a conference on relationship marketing for companies on the topic 'What companies can learn from charities'. Afterwards many of the delegates had a very different concept of what was achievable by taking a relationship marketing approach.

Getting started

The main thing to remember is that you can start small. Whether you had 6 supporters or 16, how would you get to know them and ensure that they knew you? You would probably contact them individually, and personally. You would invite them to see what you were doing and what progress you were making. Even if yours was not the type of cause with a lot to see actually, you could invite your supporters in to meet the office team or you could go and visit them. You might send them copies of press reports about your work – and when you get to know them very well, you may even send them cuttings of something of interest to them that has nothing to do with your organization at all.

If, on the other hand, you have 6,000, 60,000 or 600,000 donors, this approach may not seem a viable option and building a relationship, or any kind of personal link, is impossible. This need not be the case. Even with just one person responsible for 'donors' in your organization, this need not stop you from beginning to build relationships. As the Chinese proverb says, a journey of a thousand miles begins with a single step. And as Peppers and Rogers might say, relationship marketing can begin with a single donor.

BASIC PRINCIPLES IN PRACTICE

To establish a relationship marketing approach, the organization needs to:

■ know what it is trying to achieve with and from its supporters;
■ train the fundraising and supporter staff in the principles of relationship marketing;
■ decide how much (time and resources) the organization is going to invest in this approach;
■ decide how many supporters will be treated in this special way to start with (more can always be added);
■ take a strategic approach to implementation.

Fundamentally, the organization needs to subscribe to the view that the individual donor or supporter is more valuable than his or her last donation, and treat him or her accordingly. It is not simply a case of winning his or her loyalty but of showing him or her that loyalty can be two-way. Recognizing the implications of these facts is the start of a relationship marketing approach.

The value of a donor

As well as givers, merchandise purchasers or event attenders, donors can also be friends, allies, advocates, spokespeople, representatives and more. When I worked at the British Lung Foundation, I would visit members of the Breathe Easy club for people living with lung disease.

One particular lady lived in a small village. When I arrived she proudly announced that she had told all her family (four generations), her neighbours, her doctor and the local newsagent that I was coming to see her. In fact, by the time I got there, most of the village knew I was coming. Talking about the visit gave the lady the opportunity to talk to all these people about the charity and what it did for her. She was a more effective advocate for the British Lung Foundation than any amount of advertising and direct mail.

See the donor as an individual

However many supporters you have, it is important to see each as an individual. If the organization starts from this premise, then the donor may begin to feel appreciated as a person, instead of coded as a row of numbers on an envelope.

To this end, non-profit organizations need to give people choices as often as possible. The fundamental choice donors make is whether or not to give. As charity fundraisers, we must help to make this a positive decision. For example, a number of charities have had success from giving their donors some choice in the number of letters they receive from the charity – and then abiding by their request, even if this means reducing the number of mailings per annum from 12 to 1. What it means in practice is that the charities can save money in wasted postage and letters whilst being able to look forward to a more reliable donation each time they correspond. Because the charity reminds the donor that it is abiding by his or her wishes, the effect is to increase percentage return and income for the charity.

Communicate; do not just ask for money

In a relationship, the aim is to communicate. It is important to establish a positive dialogue, and not always to ask for money. Too often, charities make every communication about money first and information second. They also write to people in a manner that infers that the person had never heard of the charity. For those long-term supporters, it is very insulting to be written to as if completely ignorant of the work of the charity. Do not forget that many donors stay with a charity much longer than the fundraising staff.

It is also rude and shortsighted never to feed back on the outcomes of previous campaigns and the work the funds have made possible. If, in your daily life, you do something, a work colleague, a friend or family member will ask you how it went and what happened. Supporters are also asking that, and get disgruntled when the answer is another plea for money or a stand-alone and impersonal newsletter. So, think about your communications as an ongoing series, not a succession of one-off mailings.

By beginning a letter with what happened because of the last appeal, you will generate a favourable response, not always a monetary one but that of people feeling better about your organization. This is often reflected in comments on the donation form such as 'it is really nice to hear how things are going'. Not always written, but implied, is the additional line 'because you don't often hear about outcomes'.

Saying 'thank you'

A fundamental part of relationship marketing is learning how and when to say 'thank you'. Charities are notoriously bad at it. This came home to me when working for an international education charity, United World Colleges. Part of my role involved going to support the fundraising efforts of volunteer committees around the world. On one occasion in Kenya, I went to visit the PR Manager of a major company that had previously given a scholarship. My primary purpose was to say thank you and to sow the seeds for a further scholarship. After hearing my thank you, the manager said very simply, 'When people want money they are very noisy. When they get it, they go very quiet. You are the first person ever to come and say thank you for a gift.'

To start building a relationship with 'thank-yous', you could:

■ Not only thank a new donor but also send him or her a simple welcome pack about the charity so that he or she would have a better picture of what you do. You can even include a short questionnaire to help you get to know your supporter.

■ Telephone a handful of donors (regardless of amount given) at least once a month.

■ Send handwritten notes to people who give extra amounts on top of direct debits, to recognize their generosity and support.

■ Visit donors, especially those who have been supporting for a long time, to hear their perspective of the charity (this can be of great value to new staff members).

■ Invite them to come to see you at work. Even if you cannot show them work in progress, why not just invite them to your offices? One small London-based charity held an open day at its offices. Visitors had the chance to meet all the staff and hear about the work made possible by donations. They could also see that, although London based, the offices were not exactly plush.

In other words, because mail-merged, personalized letters are so easy to prepare, it is important to work that little bit harder to thank those whom you wish to nurture.

Selecting the group to focus on

Where resources are limited, it is sensible to take a strategic view and restrict the relationship building to particular groups of people. For example, you might decide to look after your regular givers in a different way from your single payment givers, or concentrate on donors giving larger amounts.

Evaluate your resources and decide where you can focus. Make sure though that those given this role understand its dimensions. They need to be comfortable talking to donors as individuals, to be sincere, to want to encourage a friendly approach without getting too close and to be passionate about the cause. In return, the supporters may come to think of you as friends. When one head of fundraising left her post, several donors wrote to thank her personally for making them feel so needed and appreciated by the charity. What better accolade can a relationship marketer have?

MEMBERSHIP SCHEMES

A membership scheme should be seen as a way to bring together a particular group of your supporters or a natural constituency – for example, all people affected by a particular medical condition. The household-name membership schemes like the National Trust and the Royal Society for the Protection of Birds (RSPB) have enormous memberships. For a small organization it can be daunting to decide where, or even whether, to start. The rest of this chapter will give some practical pointers to developing a membership scheme.

Before you start

Investing in a membership scheme is neither a quick nor a cheap option. Therefore, a proper plan needs to be developed to address the following issues:

■ Why do you want to create a club?
■ What does the organization want to get from this scheme?
■ What will its purpose be?
■ What are you going to offer members?
■ What do you want to achieve?
■ How much can you invest in the development?
■ Over what timeframe can you plan and develop it?
■ Who will run the club?

A membership scheme is more than just an expanded database. Alone, it is not necessarily a relationship marketing tool. This depends on how the scheme is applied. The first decision an organization needs to make based on these questions is, 'Is a membership scheme right for us at this time?' Such a decision may well need to be referred to the trustees, complete with the business plan for the development of the club.

Steps in planning a membership scheme

■ Define the purpose of the club.
■ Determine member benefits.
■ Consider joining and membership fees.
■ Establish the level of investment and expected return.

■ Establish promotional costs.
■ Set a realistic timeframe for achieving set goals.

The purpose of the club

A membership scheme requires people to join something. What they join must have meaning for them, whether it is to save the whale (Greenpeace), protect the environment (Friends of the Earth), give support to people with a particular medical condition (Diabetes UK) or to preserve art treasures (National Art Collections Fund). The purpose of the club should have meaning for the potential members and not just the organization. But the establishment of a scheme should be part of the strategic planning of the organization as a whole.

Determine member benefits

Potential members need to feel that they are going to get something out of their membership. For a campaigning club they might derive enough benefit from knowing that they are supporting the cause. Often, however, people want a more tangible sign of support that might range from a car sticker to special access to the premises and facilities of the charity.

When planning, you need to consider what might be appropriate to the specific nature of the club. However important it is for you to generate income for the club, it is essential also to consider the benefits to individual members.

Joining and membership fees

When joining something you expect to pay a fee. Some organizations may actually have a one-off joining fee in addition to an annual membership fee. But before deciding amounts, you might want to consider why you are setting up the scheme, who is likely to join and whether a joining fee is actually appropriate.

For example, an organization set up a club for people with a particular debilitating medical condition. It was found that those who would benefit most from the club were probably living off disability allowance and other state benefits. As a result, the trustees took the decision to set up the club with no joining fee but hoped that asking members for donations would generate income. Although not a quick income route, it suited its purpose by reaching a body of people who previously had very little support and information.

Level of investment and expected return

When setting up a membership club, the organization needs to think seriously about the level of investment that will be needed and the time frame over which outgoings are likely to exceed income. There is no hard and fast rule about level of investment, perhaps only a series of pointers to be considered – for example, a club needs an administrator, who needs a computer and a database. There will be a need for materials, club letterheads, membership cards, incentives and so on. There will also be a need for ongoing communications with members. At the very least there will need to be a request for the following year's subscription. And if the scheme is to be run on the relationship marketing model, there will need to be much more interaction. After all, a paid-up group of supporters who are advocates, activists and supporters in times of trouble, can be even more helpful than 'ordinary' supporters.

Establishing a budget for running the scheme is a crucial part of the initial planning. This needs to include costs of administering the scheme and, especially in the early days, the costs of publicizing it. Without promotion, no one will join. The methods chosen for promotion of the scheme will depend on your budget and on your target market. If you have an easy way to reach a specific niche market then there is no point in taking out full-page adverts in the national press.

Timeframe

A membership scheme should be set up as a long-term venture. It takes too much investment of time and effort to consider it as anything else. As such, the initial plans, forecasts and projections should be for at least three years. Only your figures will show if you will have broken even in that time, or have begun to generate income. But, given that this is a long-term initiative, unless you consider that you have found a very untapped and lucrative niche, the first three years should be seen as investment years. In this way, if the scheme takes off more quickly, everyone will be pleased, and, if not, there will be no surprises. You may also need to keep the core objectives of the scheme at the front of your mind – if this is providing a service to specific individuals, then return on investment may be less important.

SUMMARY

Relationship marketing and membership schemes are about building friends for the future. The aim of both is to ensure the continuity of the organization by creating a strong network of supportive individuals. In both cases, however, these are not situations that can be achieved overnight.

In this respect, it is easier to start developing a relationship marketing approach than to establish a membership scheme. But relationship marketing is not something that can be turned on and off. Once you have shown a commitment to its principles and to your donors, you only stop at your peril. Your supporters will have come to expect a certain level of service, information and feedback. If they stop getting it, they are likely to become less supportive.

When relationship marketing works, it can be beneficial to everyone. One charity fundraiser signed all the letters to covenantors and standing order donors, even though the total number rose significantly while she was in post. She would add personal handwritten postscripts on the letters to people she had met, or who had renewed a covenant or with whom she had other correspondence.

The success of this approach was measured in a variety of ways, from legacies to advocacy. Ultimately, what it meant was that donors felt a special bond with the organization that kept them supportive. That is what relationship marketing is all about.

REFERENCES

Burnett, K (1992) *Relationship Fundraising*, White Lion Press
Peppers, D and Rogers, M (1993) *The One-to-One Future*, Piatkus Books

7

Partnerships with companies

David Pettigrew

Charitable donations and activities by companies are not new. Many towns in the United Kingdom have buildings or institutions that owe their existence to the philanthropy of a business owner. The nature of company involvement has been changing, however. An increasing number of companies today see their charitable involvement as part of their business – as a way of raising profile, selling more units, building staff morale and so on. The companies' objectives, however, may differ from the charities'. Charities wanting to fundraise successfully from the corporate market need to understand the nature of that market (or, more correctly, markets). They need to realize that products or approaches will require careful matching to the company's market in question. This can make corporate fundraising seem complicated and difficult. There is no reason, however, why any charity should not work successfully in this area, with the right amount of thought and planning. This chapter covers the range of products that can be offered to companies, and looks at some of the planning that will be needed.

WHY COMPANIES WORK WITH CHARITIES

Companies work with charities for many reasons, not all of which are altruistic. Of pre-tax profit, companies in the United Kingdom give, on average, about 0.02 per cent to charity. Most commercial organizations look at a charity relationship in the same way as they would any other business relationship. There must be something in the relationship for the company. What follows outlines the benefits companies seek and those that the charity should offer when working with a company.

THE CORPORATE FUNDRAISING MIX

The corporate fundraising mix can be broken down into the following areas:

■ staff or employee fundraising;
■ cause-related marketing;
■ sponsorship;
■ events;
■ donations;
■ payroll giving.

Staff fundraising

Every company relies on a hardworking and committed workforce for its success. In order to achieve a motivated and productive workforce, many organizations spend a lot of resources building team spirit and commitment to the company. One additional way for a company to achieve these results is through a successful staff fundraising campaign. Staff fundraising is an opportunity for a company to work with a charity and use its employees as the vehicle to raise money.

The principal benefits of staff fundraising campaigns are:

■ An excellent method of building team spirit and company loyalty.
■ Bringing staff together from different departments working towards a common goal. Valuable improvements in cross-

departmental communication often follow staff fundraising campaigns.

■ Linking to a specific event or clear financial target (for example, staff fundraising is an ideal way to celebrate a company anniversary).
■ Providing ideal media opportunities locally, nationally and in the specialist and trade media.
■ Helping a company to demonstrate its credentials as a good corporate citizen.
■ Low cost but bringing high returns for the company and a very high value to the charities.

The most successful campaigns tend to have a matched funding agreement from the company. This is where the company agrees to match all or a percentage of the money raised by the employees. (For example, for every £1 raised by staff the company will give another £1.) This motivates staff because they can see direct support for the campaign from the very top of the company and that the campaign is inclusive.

Cause-related marketing

Cause-related marketing (CRM) has been with us for some years. The first major successful campaign was run by American Express in 1983 (see case study below).

CRM has been defined by Business in the Community as:

A commercial activity by which businesses and charities or causes form a partnership with each other to market an image, product or service for mutual benefit.

These partnerships involve companies using a campaign linked to a charity to increase sales and raise money for that charity. Clearly there must be good reason for both parties to enter into such a partnership. These can be defined as:

■ **benefits to the company:**
 - increased business;
 - positive PR;
 - increased awareness;
 - seen as a socially responsible company;

- staff motivation;
- increase in customer loyalty;
- new customers;
- access to the charity's network (considerable in some cases).
■ **benefits to the charity:**
  - more of their client group helped;
  - funds raised;
  - partnership with a professional organization;
  - shared knowledge and learning;
  - raise awareness of the work of the charity.

There are five rules that need to be remembered when looking at a CRM promotion:

1. **Ensure a natural fit.** When putting a company and a charity together it is important to make sure that there is a natural fit between the organizations and that the buying public can clearly see that fit. The consumer is a sophisticated animal and can see through poorly designed campaigns that are perceived as attempts by a company simply to make money on the back of the charity. As a rule of thumb, if it sounds forced or unnatural, that is how the consumer will see it.
2. **Shared market audience.** The target of a CRM campaign is the consumer. In a successful campaign, the charity and the company will have similar target groups of supporters and consumers. This means that the campaign is mutually supportive because those who buy the product will also empathize with the charity and vice versa. It is worth bearing in mind, however, that a charity approaching a company with an idea for a CRM campaign will need to show understanding of two markets – the company itself and its customers. This is where research becomes particularly important.
3. **Mutually beneficial.** The campaign must benefit both parties as equally as possible and must be seen to do so. In a situation where the company stands to benefit considerably more than the charity, the consumer will lose confidence in the company and could question the integrity of the charity for entering into a dubious partnership. It is also an unfortunate possibility that such an arrangement will cast a pall over other charities working in a similar area.

4. **Issue or cause as a motivator.** It is important to understand that it is not the charity *per se* that will sell a product, but the issue or cause associated with it. For example, in the case of childcare charity NCH, it is not the name that provides the motivator but the information about the problems the charity exists to solve and the way it goes about doing that.

5. **Professional account management.** A commercial organization expects to deliver its product effectively and efficiently. It needs to have confidence in those who represent the charity. This comes from professional account management. By running our 'business' in a professional fashion, we gain credibility and are seen as able to deliver our half of the partnership. This does not mean that 'small charities need not apply', but that whoever deals with companies must adopt a professional approach.

One of the attractions of CRM to companies is that it is a measurable activity. A benefit must be measurable and there must be a gain for the company in performance.

These measurable points are known as Key Performance Indicators (KPI) and they can be summarized as follows:

■ Amount raised.
■ Measured effect on:
  – sales;
  – volume;
  – customers.
■ Media/PR coverage:
  – national;
  – local;
  – specialist/trade.
■ Impact on:
  – reputation;
  – awareness;
  – image.
■ Satisfaction levels:
  – customer;
  – employees;
  – stakeholder.
■ Impact on:
  – community;
  – competition.

Sponsorship

Company sponsorship of charitable work very often involves providing the backing for an event such as a ball or something a bit more unusual such as a 'sleepout' in aid of homelessness. The advantage of sponsorship is that it allows the company to pick up costs the charity would otherwise have to bear. Events can be expensive and, in terms of finance, time and effort, are not always cost effective. Sponsorship is often the difference between a financially successful event and a failure.

Other areas to consider for sponsorship are annual reports, publications and general materials. It is worth remembering that the company will expect certain returns for its sponsorship. These will include prominence for the company name/branding at an event or in the publication. However, charities should be aware of the value of their sponsorship opportunities. They should not undervalue and sell themselves short. Remember to price these opportunities competitively.

Events

Corporate events involving charities cover a wide range of possibilities from balls to sponsored walks. Many charities offer employees the opportunity to take part in bike rides, white water rafting and marathons in far-flung and exotic places as part of the wider staff fundraising programme.

The nature of the event chosen is not the only key to success. The most exciting event in the world is of no benefit if it does not earn the charity income that can be used for its work.

Events, even those carried out in conjunction with a company, must be properly planned in terms of income, expenditure, net profit, time and effort. An event needs to have a good cost to income ratio in order to be considered a success.

Donations

Corporate donations remain a part of fundraising for charities. Very often, a donation is the start of a long-lasting relationship that may lead on to other types of fundraising with a company. Like other types of fundraising, however, they require more than just a letter asking for a donation, then sitting back and waiting for the cheque.

A company that donates to a charity still expects a benefit in return, whether it is positive PR, an opportunity to join a board of trustees or some other form of recognition. Remember to look at the value of the donation against what is being 'offered' in return to ensure the charity also gets value for money.

Payroll giving

Payroll Giving (PRG) is a tax efficient way for employees to give to charity through their employer's payroll. As gifts are made before tax, the value of the donation is effectively topped up by the government. The UK government will add an additional 10 per cent to every donation made in this way from the year 2000 to 2004 as part of a campaign to encourage PRG.

Correctly done, PRG is an effective way of fundraising as it provides a long-term commitment by the donor. The average life of a PRG donation is five to seven years. This type of commitment permits effective forecasting of income levels .

PRG campaigns too often rely on a few scattered leaflets in an office or a poster pinned to a bulletin board. Sadly, these are not the most efficient methods of promoting PRG as they do not effectively engage the audience.

The key to a successful campaign is to persuade company management to allow you to speak to employees at team meetings. This affords the opportunity for direct face-to-face fundraising. This technique was successfully carried out by NCH Action for Children with Kwik-Fit Insurance Services (see case study below).

NEW BUSINESS DEVELOPMENT

For any charity, the development of new corporate business is crucial. While it is a fantastic achievement to win that big corporate account, it will need to be replaced at some time in the future. Charity of the Year promotions, for example, are by their very nature temporary arrangements. To fill that gap it is important to plan well ahead when considering new business.

Figure 7.1 and the notes below give an idea of the process for new business development. The figure should be viewed as a guide and can be 'cherry-picked' to support a charity's own needs.

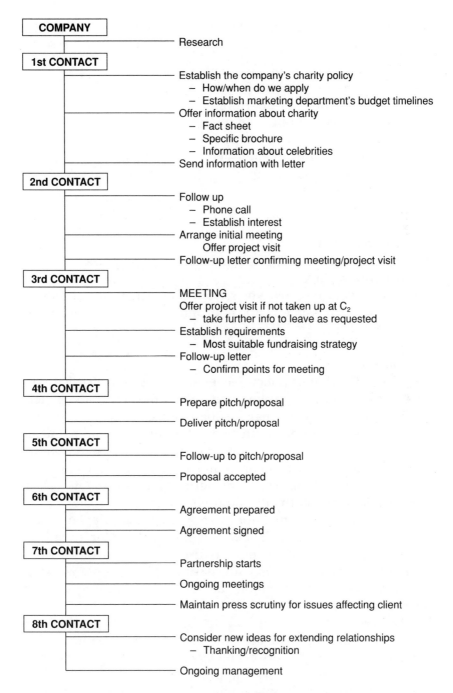

COMPANY
— Research

1st CONTACT
— Establish the company's charity policy
  - How/when do we apply
  - Establish marketing department's budget timelines
— Offer information about charity
  - Fact sheet
  - Specific brochure
  - Information about celebrities
— Send information with letter

2nd CONTACT
— Follow up
  - Phone call
  - Establish interest
— Arrange initial meeting
    Offer project visit
— Follow-up letter confirming meeting/project visit

3rd CONTACT
— MEETING
Offer project visit if not taken up at C_2
  - take further info to leave as requested
— Establish requirements
  - Most suitable fundraising strategy
— Follow-up letter
  - Confirm points for meeting

4th CONTACT
— Prepare pitch/proposal
— Deliver pitch/proposal

5th CONTACT
— Follow-up to pitch/proposal
— Proposal accepted

6th CONTACT
— Agreement prepared
— Agreement signed

7th CONTACT
— Partnership starts
— Ongoing meetings
— Maintain press scrutiny for issues affecting client

8th CONTACT
— Consider new ideas for extending relationships
  - Thanking/recognition
— Ongoing management

Figure 7.1

New business development process notes

1. The company chosen can come from the following sources:
   - it is known to support charitable work;
   - an opportunity is spotted in the media;
   - from a networking opportunity;
   - specific interest from a fundraiser;
   - has a connection with a supporter;
   - an approach from an interested company/agency.
2. Research can be carried out using the following methods:
   - business journals;
   - the Internet;
   - the press;
   - research team;
   - company information, eg annual accounts/reports;
   - networking links.

   As part of your research, you should consider all ethical considerations and possible conflicts of interest with an existing or potential client.

First contact

3. Establish the charity policy. Never send an unsolicited letter to a company. Most companies, particularly the bigger and better-known ones, receive many submissions for support every week. Most are simply addressed to the company and not to an individual. Often called 'round robin letters', these proposals are sent out to many companies and are not tailored to any individual organization. They are normally addressed to 'Dear Sir/Madam' and normally end up in the bin.

   When making the first approach, pick up the telephone and call the company. Establish who is the right person to talk to and use this as an opportunity to discover what he or she does and how he or she works with charities. Most people working with voluntary organizations are only too happy to explain what they do.

   The great advantage of making this contact is that you and your organization will be remembered when sending your proposal to the right person and tailored to that organization.

   Each company a charity approaches will have a different policy towards charitable giving. Some will have published criteria for support and a charity committee meeting regularly.

Others will have a nominated charity of the year. Where a company does have a Charity of the Year (COY) you should ascertain the following:
– when does the annual relationship start (eg January)?
– when should you apply?
– what is the application process?
Even if they are not looking for a charity of the year, there may well be other ways you can work with them. These should be considered and offered up and would include any of the possibilities from the fundraising mix.

4. Marketing department's timelines. If the marketing department is targeted, find out the timescales to which they work. It could well be that a good CRM campaign may take a couple of years to achieve once all the relationship building is considered. Therefore, plan ahead!

5. Follow up with information. After that initial contact, follow up with a letter and relevant information about the charity. Do it the same day and they will not have time to forget you. Do not send too much at this stage as it would not be read – unless of course you have been asked to make a specific proposal at this time.

Second contact

6. Follow up. Follow up your letter with a telephone call to establish if there is interest. If the company is interested, try to arrange a meeting. Ensure you speak to the right people. If not, find out who the right person is.

   Remember, just because someone says 'no', he or she may not necessarily mean no for all time. No may mean any of the following:
   – No, I am not interested now but I may be in a few months.
   – No, I am not interested but I know someone else in the company who may be.
   – No, this particular proposal is not quite what I need, give me some other ideas more closely linked to my business/staff.
   If a meeting is arranged, follow up with a letter of confirmation.

Third contact

7. The first meeting. This is your chance to make an impact! It is a chance to explore the supporter's requirements and

establish what might work best for them. It is the first chance to sell both your organization and yourself and 'first impressions count'.

Once you have established a rapport, look at the type of fundraising strategies from the fundraising mix open to you and the client:

- staff or employee fundraising;
- CRM;
- sponsorship;
- events;
- donations;
- payroll giving.

Then try to persuade the client to take up a project visit. Fundraisers can talk at length about the work their charity does but there is no better way to sell it than for a supporter actually to see it at first hand.

This meeting should be as much about information gathering about the company (policies; culture; budgets; timescales; objectives; current and future plans) as an information session about your charity. Ask lots of questions about them and be interested in them. Remember – 'flattery will get you every-where'! (If you manage to secure a meeting at this stage – great, but some companies may want to see some 'ideas in writing' before agreeing to a meeting.)

8. After the meeting, follow up with a letter and any further information promised at the meeting. Confirm any points from the meeting and your agreed actions.

Fourth contact

9. Having held a successful meeting you may now be expected to prepare a formal presentation or proposal. This may be read or attended not just by your contact, but also by others in the organization. It has to be professional. If you require assistance from colleagues, ensure that you get it. If you are making a presentation, take a member of your operations staff to cover the operational points if this is appropriate. Practise your pitch before you go in front of someone who has had little or no involvement in the planning (clarity is key – make sure jargon has been eliminated). Remember to leave a hard copy of your pitch when giving a presentation. Alternatively, the company/contact may

suggest you meet another department or person before any formal proposal is required. This may happen several times.

Fifth contact

10. Follow up your pitch or proposal covering any points arising from it or any points the client wishes resolved following the presentation.
11. Your proposal is accepted! If this is in writing – fine! If over the telephone, write to the client thanking them. This is one way of ensuring written confirmation of their acceptance. Often there will be amendments to your original proposal, or caveats and conditions imposed.

Sixth contact

12. You should now arrange a meeting to prepare the basis of an agreement between the two parties. You should ensure that an agreement exists between the parties prior to launching your relationship. This protects both the charity and the company. Both organizations have expectations from the relationship; this agreement allows both to have those expectations met.

Seventh contact

13. Your partnership starts, but this is only the beginning!
14. For a relationship to be successful, ongoing professional account management is vital. You must ensure the client continues to be managed as professionally as possible.
15. Maintain an interest in the client's business. Be aware of issues affecting them, like mergers or takeovers that often appear in the press. This will help you avoid being caught out! Be aware too of their work routines and timetables. The day before the annual report goes to press is not a good day for a chat with the head of marketing, for example.

Eighth contact

16. Once your partnership has started, it is time to think of ways of extending it. In the first instance, this will be influenced by your account management. After about six months, consider how to move the relationship forward using other methods to develop the partnership over the longer term. Also, consider

relevant and appropriate thanking and recognition opportunities.

17. And finally, ongoing management is vital to your success. Remember, if this client is happy, they will tell others. Networking leads to new business.

HALIFAX AND NCH ACTION FOR CHILDREN

Introduction

Following Halifax's de-mutualisation, the bank wanted to raise awareness of its Young Savers Account to new and existing customers.

Objectives

▨ to encourage customers both existing and new to open a children's savings account;

▨ to raise £20,000 for NCH Action for Children in a cost effective and simple way;

▨ to raise awareness of Halifax's ongoing support of NCH Action for Children;

▨ to generate positive PR around the activity.

Mechanic

▨ For every Little Xtra account opened between 24th November 1997 and 5th January 1998, Halifax donated £1.00 to NCH Action for Children.

▨ Colourful point-of-sale material was designed featuring Halifax and NCH Action for Children branding.

▨ Halifax ran a competition linked to the promotion that invited children to design a Christmas scene. Prizes included a family holiday in Florida, mountain bikes and Toys R Us gift vouchers.

Results

▨ During the promotional period, 29,638 accounts were opened.

▨ Over 2,800 entries were received for the Design a Christmas Scene competition.

▓ There was widespread publicity in the local and national newspapers.
▓ The promotion raised £29,638 for NCH Action for Children.

During the previous Christmas period (1996) Halifax ran a similar promotion but without a charity link. A third more accounts were opened during the NCH Action for Children promotion.

AMERICAN EXPRESS

American Express (Amex) is credited with the first important CRM deal in 1983. The company raised US $1.7 million for the restoration of the Statue of Liberty through card use. The three-month programme was used by Amex as an alternative to being a formal sponsor of the restoration programme and was aimed at increasing card use, increasing new card applications and raising money for the fund. The company agreed to donate US $1 to the fund for every card transaction and US $5 for every new card application. The scheme produced a 27 per cent increase in card usage and a 17 per cent increase in new member applications.

Amex has followed up this pioneering activity with other projects, such as the Charge against Hunger programme that ran in the US for four years until 1996. Three cents for each card transaction in the busy fourth quarter of the year went to the US domestic anti-hunger charity Share our Strength. The programme was well publicized and raised US $20 million for the charity. The company says the arrangement worked in terms of increased card usage too. Grants were distributed across 50 states to 600 organizations.

KWIK-FIT INSURANCE

Introduction

Based in Uddingston, Kwik-Fit Insurance Services started operating in 1995 with approximately 50 employees. Today with over

800 employees, it was recently voted best call centre in Scotland and fourth overall in the United Kingdom. They invest heavily in the training and development of their employees and were awarded an Investors in People Award in 1999. As part of Kwik-Fit Insurance Services' community involvement and commitment to their employees, NCH Action for Children was given the opportunity to promote payroll giving in September 1999 with very successful results.

The key to the success of this campaign was the opportunity for face-to-face fundraising with employees. This was possible due to the excellent relationship built up between Kwik-Fit Insurance Services and NCH Action for Children.

Objectives

▓ to introduce payroll giving to employees at Kwik-Fit Insurance Services;
▓ to encourage involvement in the local community through a simple fundraising mechanic;
▓ to generate a regular and predictable income for NCH Action for Children.

Mechanic

A two-week pre-publicity period within Kwik-Fit Insurance Services gave NCH Action for Children the opportunity to heighten awareness of their work in Scotland. This involved an NCH Action for Children video playing in the staff restaurant, posters, balloons, T-shirts, e-mail advertising and an internal magazine feature on payroll giving.

After the pre-publicity period, a team of five from NCH Action for Children went in to Kwik-Fit Insurance Services and presented to all employees. Groups of five to ten employees listened to the short five-minute presentation on the work of NCH Action for Children and the advantages of PRG.

They were asked to sign up to the scheme using the NCH Action for Children mandate form provided. As an incentive, those who signed up were entered into a prize draw where the winner had lunch with a celebrity.

NCH Action for Children staff took only five days to present to over 800 staff with minimum disruption to each working day.

Results

- The target uptake for the campaign was exceeded with over 10 per cent of employees signed up to the scheme.
- The average amount pledged was £7 a month, giving NCH Action for Children a regular annual income of over £7,500. The average lifetime of a payroll giver is five to seven years.
- Kwik-Fit Insurance Services staff were introduced to PRG as a quick and easy way to support not only NCH Action for Children but also any other charity of their choice.
- Local PR coverage for Kwik-Fit Insurance.

8

PR-led marketing communications

Olly Grender

INTRODUCTION

PR is not an exact science

Neither marketing nor public relations are exact sciences. Advertising often has clearly identifiable audiences, means of measuring success and a clear target. Public relations requires the same. Both need creativity and imagination that will capture the attention of a target audience for that rare moment in their otherwise busy day. Public relations in the not-for-profit sector can be as large as a £6 million budget to increase awareness and as small as the chief executive's contingency budget. What follows are some examples and thoughts on how to see the 'wood for the trees' when working on public relations in the not-for-profit sector.

If you cannot spend on advertising and intend to use the media for a public relations campaign then you must understand that this is a medium with a life of its own. Journalists are under no obligation to run your story your way. You are relying on a third party to tell your story. This increases the risk. On the other hand, while you cannot guarantee the message, if you succeed you can reach very large audiences and have a similar impact to spending on advertising.

Do not neglect the reactive operation

An important part of a public relations operation is being ready to react to other stories. You may have spent a year planning for a promotional activity and the week before D-Day a story breaks that is clearly in your sector. Do not miss that moment to go for it. There is always a danger of losing sight of what the real world is talking about because you have a mailing that must get out to 800 journalists and you are in the middle of a row with the printers. However limited your resources, you need to decide quickly whether or not you have a choice.

What follows is about preparing for a launch and preparing good positive 'proactive' public relations campaigns. But do not lose sight of the real world. If the nine o'clock news is running a story, no amount of appearances on 24-hour news the following week is going to compensate for the lost opportunity. Being swift with a reaction is important. At Shelter they had the luxury of people who wanted to be on TV and did not care what time of the day, or night, it was. There are horror stories of other charities that do not have that luxury. If your chief executive is not prepared to react swiftly to a story and get into a studio, be ruthless and find someone who is. It is worth identifying several 'good talkers' to keep in reserve for moments like that.

Do not forget risk strategies

Reactive work also includes planning for stories that you would rather did not happen. If there is anything at all happening in your organization which you think will lead to adverse publicity, then prepare for it. Prepare a line and agree it with the relevant people. It is of equal importance to make sure you have a system to flag up negative issues that might be 'hiding' in remote parts of the organization. Ensure that you have established who will brief journalists, who in the organization will be responsible for finding out what the true story is, and who will direct the operation. If you have time, ensure that the relevant person gets media training. If not, then rehearse with him or her yourself. Write an action plan then put the file away. And above all, whatever you do, tell the truth or those journalists will come back to haunt you.

PR within a changing environment

If you are producing a full communications strategy, allow room for flexibility. The environment around your issue is constantly changing. Nearly all of those changes are outside your control. For example, on some issues focus has moved to the role of the 'consumer' in affecting public opinion. If you are still concentrating on the role of 'activist', you will not capture the moment or the attention of the media. If you are already involved in public relations work, you will know that journalists tend to follow trends at the speed of light. Then they will be onto the next thing. Adjust your plans accordingly whilst holding onto your main themes and positioning of the organization.

PLANNING

What do you want to do?

Do you want to publicize an event, change opinion on a controversial issue or do you simply want to increase knowledge of the organization? Ask yourself whether perhaps you want to raise money or convince the government or a local authority on a particular issue. All these things can be achieved through a good public relations campaign. But be sparing with your goals and try to be realistic about expectations.

Identify target audiences and desired outcomes

Marketing targets tend to start first with the audiences you want to reach. It is important to escape the generalized terms 'public awareness' and 'the general public' as often as possible. If you have to use these categories, strip down exactly who your audiences are. They may be your client group, your membership, politicians and 'opinion formers'. (Marketing to opinion formers is covered specifically in Chapter 4.) By identifying your target audiences, you should be able to identify the medium that you intend to use. This decision, and not just the media your board members happen to be familiar with, should drive your decisions. The trade press, for example, is often more likely to be effective in reaching your audiences than the national press. If you work with the specialist media, you will also be dealing with journalists who have a more detailed understanding of your story.

Identify your resources – human and financial

Public relations can include a significant amount of expenditure. Or it can use all the people you have as a resource. Shelter launched a 24-hour helpline in December 1998. There was a budget of £250,000 to advertise the service. An amount of money like that will not reach everyone, so Shelter elected to advertise in selected areas only in order to reach potential clients. The spin-off was anecdotal evidence that key opinion formers woke up to the real practical work Shelter does. However, this is a mere drop in the ocean when trying to advertise a service to the whole of the United Kingdom. If an organization will require advertising spend in the future, start putting it into the annual budget now, do not wait for the choice to become whether or not to cut back on spending on a service in order to pay for advertisements. It is worth considering, carefully, the one controversial advert that will result in a PR spin-off. (Examples of advertising that have generated editorial coverage include Save the Children's birthday advertisement featuring the Princess Royal and, more controversially, the Barnardo's advertisements juxtaposing children and drugs, prison and homelessness.)

Identify best medium – again related to outcome

Having identified key audiences, identify how to reach them. It may be through an annual report, a mailing; it may be through an advertising campaign. Make sure that you identify that best vehicle. For many welfare and developing world organizations, good target audiences are churchgoers. They are often active citizens prepared to write to the local MP or newspaper on your behalf. Again, this decision is taken in conjunction with the outcome that you want which relies on positioning of the organization and the strategy.

Positioning of the organization

Decide how you want your organization to be viewed. Try if possible to get ownership of that view within the organization. Do you want to be seen as 'radical – hard edged'? Do you want to be seen as thoughtful – research based? If your organization is large, there is a danger that the answer will be 'yes' to both. Try at least to solve this conundrum within the press office or communications team. A good exercise is to get everyone to write a mock editorial in a broadsheet newspaper about how the organization is viewed. Often writing how you would want the commentary to appear gives you a good idea about how to position the organization or the public relations campaign. Whatever you do, do not put a 'spin' on the description of the organization unless it is sustainable.

Have a strategy attached

Once you have answered some of the questions above, write a strategy for the media event or public relations campaign. You may need help in the form of academic research. You may need policy input or information about what your organization does. If you want any of those things, then first try to establish a clear strategy with your organization.

'Meat and two veg approach'

In the world of charity, the 'big picture' ends often obscure the means. Do not forget the basics. Unless someone is prepared to do a mailing, do a ring round, fax through the information, do the basic work, any amount of planning will count for nothing. A superb strategy will not be borne out unless someone has written a good newsworthy media release. Always check that someone is first putting the information in the right diaries. Finding out you have no spokespeople in the country days before a major launch can eliminate much potential coverage. This sounds obvious, but it is surprising just how often these basics are neglected.

'Short and dirty'

If you are looking for a small public relations hit there is nothing wrong with the short and dirty. Sometimes some of the best publicity will come from just that. Out of research, it is possible to produce smaller, more 'poppy' pieces of research. For example, at Shelter a pamphlet was written about fathers who have nowhere for their children to visit them. It had some anecdotal evidence. The leaflet hit the media at a time when divorce was prevalent in people's minds. Called *What If It's Raining*, the publication generated national media coverage.

Think small

In the voluntary sector people often want to change the world tomorrow. Part of your role as a public relations officer is to set achievable targets. Large amounts of money can often be spent on a video news release, for example (footage, interviews and information on broadcast quality videotape), when an audio news release (the same sort of thing but for radio) is cheaper to produce and will be used by most local radio stations.

Plan for evaluation at the beginning

Find ways to measure your target audience's response. That could be done by quantitative polling and tracking changing opinion amongst target audiences. Media monitoring is another way of measuring success, but make sure that measuring does not get out of proportion to the real work. (Evaluation is tackled in more detail in Chapter 11.) Targets in the media should be clear. If you want that helpline number to be in the top paragraph, that is a clear target. This is an important element of seeing how effective your work has been and demonstrating to those who allocate the budgets whether or not they are getting good value for money.

PARTNERSHIPS

Using partnerships – corporate and quirky

Partnership is a buzzword almost everywhere, unless you are working in one. Choose partnerships carefully and set ground rules at an early stage. A partnership could, for example, be some *pro bono* advertising by an agency for a charity. This can be fraught with problems unless at the outset the agency is clear what the organization wants to achieve. Shelter once received some *pro bono* work on an advert where the creatives in that agency had a very clear idea about homelessness. This did not coincide with Shelter's view of homelessness. Instead of an easy freebie and the hopes of an advertising award for the agency, there were months of negotiations and a disproportionate amount of time spent in persuasion on both sides.

On the other hand, a partnership with the corporate sector can often produce rewarding public relations results. An example is the partnership between the RNID (Royal National Institute for Deaf People) and the UK Offshore Operators Association Limited (UKOOA) to launch a campaign entitled *Indecent Exposure* (a campaign to highlight noise in the workplace) in March 1999. The objectives were to raise general awareness of the dangers of noise in the workplace, to put pressure on employers, to make employees aware of the dangers, to enlist the support of MPs and to recruit a sponsor that shares the vision.

The RNID carried out research with the TUC. They identified key target media and produced information materials such as leaflets for employers and employees. They evaluated all of their media coverage, which reached over 28 million adults. People researched were exposed to the campaign coverage on average 1.9 times. They carefully selected and targeted their media within the health and safety trade press.

On the day of the launch 87 radio stations broadcast details including the *Today Programme* (BBC Radio 4) and the *Jimmy Young Show* (BBC Radio 2). Eight national newspapers covered the story including a full-page feature in the *Sunday Express*.

UKOOA sponsored the event. The organization 'had a general appreciation of the fact that reputation was a function of behaviour and communication... (and) also wanted to explore the possibilities of being seen to change behaviour by communications'. Sponsorship of such campaigns often gives commercial organizations a softer image and gets them in front of opinion-forming audiences that they might not otherwise reach.

With the media

An alternative is to form a partnership with the media, which at least guarantees coverage of the public relations campaign, although this might put off other newspapers. One example of such a partnership was the Strip 4 Shelter partnership between Shelter and *The Sun*. Whilst many would baulk at such a partnership, the voluntary sector must be ruthless and professional in pursuing the ultimate aim of the organization. If that aim is to raise money in order to campaign for homeless people, then the largest possible audience should be reached. *The Sun* is capable of providing that audience. Shelter worked with Freud Communications, an external public relations firm, to negotiate the deal. It resulted in extensive coverage of a fun idea to raise money for the charity, which was to encourage people to pay £2 to wear a football strip to work on Friday 24 September. School pupils paid 50p for the chance to wear their strip to classes. *The Sun* encouraged its readers to donate to Shelter through their workplace. The campaign raised £250,000 in its first year. Evaluation has also shown that it generated £1.35 million worth of coverage with 166 million opportunities to hear, see or read about Strip 4 Shelter.

If you are a smaller charity, local newspapers are keen to get a strong local angle. You may be just the charity they are looking for to campaign on behalf of over the Christmas period. You may have local information that they would love to cover. The very small free newspapers are often in search of decent copy. An exclusive public relations campaign through their pages may suit them well.

Of course journalists have a different agenda from your own, so be clear about the remit of the partnership. Also, accept that sometimes you might not control the agenda as much as you would like.

Core v centre, or do not forget the regions

Do not forget that regional newspapers and radio have a very high circulation and, according to polling research, people are more likely to believe them than the nationals. When the RNID launched its *Indecent Exposure* campaign, it had regional spokespeople ready and trained. Likewise, launches should have regional breakdowns of every figure, which almost guarantees coverage. Be careful, however, to make sure your regional figures are robust. They should be large enough to sound significant.

Your most important partnership – with the client

If you are a not-for-profit organization that works with, or campaigns for, a particular group of people, then clients are your lifeline. Every journalist you call, every time you launch a piece of research, every photo opportunity you hold, will generate requests for case histories. For some organizations, this can be very difficult. Some practitioners find this problematic. But there is no doubt that nothing is more powerful than hearing the story straight from the individual affected.

Firstly, draw up an agreement between yourself and the client. Make sure that they are prepared to appear in the media and fully understand what this entails. Make sure that their practitioner contact is part of the process. As an organization, you are seeking respect for your client group from the public so you need to show them the same respect. And always thank them afterwards. It is worth adding the 'thank-yous' to your planning list at the outset, as in the aftermath of a hectic few days it is easy to relax and forget this basic courtesy.

For some organizations, finding clients willing to speak can be very hard. For Shelter, many former homeless people did not want to revisit that part of their past. Likewise, people with mental health problems are reluctant to expose themselves to such scrutiny. Journalists will rarely understand this point. One way to get round this is to interview the client yourself, but many journalists will not accept that as an option. You can, though, explore using other names and photographs that do not directly identify their subjects.

NATURAL TENSIONS

The public affairs tension

Your public affairs agenda and your public relations agenda may often come into conflict. If possible, try to resolve this in the planning stage. Whilst you may have a very clear agenda about exposing the horrors on a particular issue, you must always be aware of whether this cuts across your own lobbying efforts. This is a constant tightrope which most of the voluntary sector find themselves walking.

If you are trying to reach decision makers and you have a hard-hitting public relations campaign ready to go, it may be worth doing behind-the-scenes lobbying first before it goes out. It is important to avoid the prospect of your decision maker becoming entrenched because doing anything else would be viewed by the media as a 'climbdown'. This applies as much nationally as locally.

Always measure the bottom line – does your action improve things for your client group?

Tensions with the media

As a result of the 1997 change of government and new campaigning atmosphere, for some not-for-profit organizations there are tensions with the media. Some organizations are not prepared to give a knee-jerk reaction to breaking stories. They may also cut out the media altogether and try to get to the government directly. For some journalists this reduces their role of being 'on the side of the angels'. For the previous 20 years, that had been a natural order. The majority of the charity world united with the media against the government. The picture is now more confusing and belief in who are the angels has also become more confused. For example, news programmes are now more sceptical of not-for-profit sector information. Information about Brent Spar from Greenpeace is a high-profile example of where journalists, whether rightly or wrongly, felt that they had been misinformed. They are more rigorous about the information that they receive. One example will illustrate this. Under the last two editorships of the *Today Programme*, fewer charity launches have been used.

Competition and collaboration

'Everyone working together' is attractive to the media, the public and the policy makers. Therefore, it is worth pursuing. Sometimes it can be a confusing issue to pursue when competition is encouraged everywhere else. However, in the charity sector, competition tends to be viewed as unhealthy. Shelter and Crisis worked together. Crisis provided immediate access for homeless people over the Christmas period and Shelter provided longer-term advice in order to ensure that people had options other than returning to the street. It is early days but that kind of partnership is well received in public relations terms. Another example is the operation of the Disasters Emergency Committee, which pulls together major aid agencies at times of high profile disaster.

Synergy with fundraising objectives

We are living in an age where people make snap judgements based on limited information. That information may be received through a variety of media. If you have planned, agreed the positioning of your organization and agreed a strategy across all the communications outlets within your organization then you may be all right. However, if one part of your organization is dedicated to cause-related marketing (the charity on the milk carton), while there is a direct mail campaign from another department, while you are about to launch into a high-profile public relations campaign, do ensure that those messages are coherent. (See Chapter 12 on integration and Chapter 7 on corporate fundraising and cause-related marketing.)

THE FUTURE

New media

Studies suggest that people have limited time to make a judgement about an organization. At the same time, the media for information are massively expanding. Visit any Web site of a charity and you will see for yourself. If you are part of a small or growing charity then start, like advertising, to budget for this now. (Chapter 5 focuses on the Internet.)

CONCLUSION

The challenges for future charities are endless. The charitable sector is now part of an industry worth billions of pounds. Like every sector, there is good practice and bad practice. The media are wise to this but public relations through the media is still a highly effective way of getting your message across.

Points to bear in mind

- Do not neglect reactive work.
- Do not forget risk strategies.
- Establish what the outcome should be and how you want to position the organization.
- Identify your resources – human and financial.
- 'Meat and two veg approach' – do not forget the basics.
- Plan for evaluation at the beginning.
- Use partnerships, media and corporate.
- Watch out for areas of tension with the media, with fundraisers.

9

Events and conferences as a marketing tool

Howard Barclay

Any music or sports fan knows that viewing a concert or match on TV simply does not compare to being part of the audience and watching it live. The atmosphere and experience of actually being there can sweep you off your feet, have you enthralled and totally caught up in what is happening in front of you. In short, you become part of the experience rather than just an onlooker.

No other element of the marketing mix can evoke such emotion and involvement as well as generating a lasting effect that the audience carries away. It is, therefore, arguably the most effective way to communicate a message or brand.

Live events can be especially effective within the charity sector that relies heavily on winning hearts and minds in order to achieve its objectives and often has the challenge of communicating emotive and sensitive messages.

Live events can take many forms including conferences, exhibitions, awards ceremonies, auctions, press conferences, campaign launches, annual general meetings, fashion shows and gala dinners to name but a few. They all provide an opportunity to market your brand and communicate your message first hand to a selected audience. The bulk of this chapter is about organizing a single, major event. Many of the principles, however, are also relevant to smaller events and to taking part in other people's events.

PLANNING YOUR EVENT

The following key elements should always be included in the planning of any event, large or small.

Objectives

When starting out on planning an event, most organizations or individuals know their reasons for holding the event but are not always clear about its objectives. It is imperative that the objectives are clearly defined and agreed upon at the outset, as the objectives will dictate many of the elements that make up the event. Also, post-event you should measure the success of the event against your objectives.

The most common objectives of a live event are to communicate a specific message or generate revenue, but others include:

■ marketing the brand;
■ obtaining feedback;
■ promoting awareness of topics or issues;
■ setting targets;
■ motivating your audience;
■ networking with colleagues and exchanging information;
■ rewarding individuals;
■ recognizing achievements.

Audience

Identifying the people you want in your audience, and the size of audience you want in order to meet your objectives, is crucial. If your aim is to raise funds, large numbers may be your priority. For a campaign launch, however, a small number of carefully selected influential opinion formers may be more appropriate. Great importance should be placed on identifying your desired audience and ensuring their attendance.

Budget

Clearly, budget will be one of the most significant factors in determining the format of your event, but whatever the size of the event a cost/profit projection should always be carried out at the outset. Too often the most wonderful event that is enjoyed by all fails to make money. If your objective was to raise funds, this is clearly a problem.

As minimizing expenditure is always high on the list of priorities for a charity sector organization, you should consider negotiating with suppliers to provide free or reduced-cost services and facilities as a 'donation' or in return for recognition or sponsorship throughout the event, if appropriate.

Resources

Identify the resources available to you in planning, organizing and managing your event. It is usually difficult for staff to be taken away from their main job for lengthy periods so you might consider using volunteers or an external agency. However, you should ensure that they are adequately skilled and experienced in the areas you assign them to, that they are managed and that appropriate training, insurance, health and safety requirements are in place.

Theme

The theme, style and tone of your event will usually be dictated by the objectives but should always reflect your organization's core values and *raison d'être*. Ensure that your message does not get 'lost'.

Venue

The size of your audience will dictate several features of the event venue, particularly location and size. You should consider accessibility both locally and nationally, as appropriate, and the cost and availability of different methods of transport for your audience.

When looking for a venue it is often advisable to use the services of a venue finding agency (see below). It is a good idea to choose a venue that can accommodate an event in excess of your audience size so that your delegates feel comfortable and not cramped or claustrophobic. A room with a large number of people will soon get quite hot and stuffy, so one with air-conditioning is always preferable. Similarly, ensure that there is adequate heating in your venue. This is particularly relevant if the venue is an open space or marquee.

Aisle widths for visitors in an exhibition or conference auditorium should always be a minimum of two metres wide to ensure they comply with current health and safety regulations. Keep this in mind when looking at a venue and how it will be laid out.

When considering a potential venue it is equally important to view other areas that will be used in addition to the main event area. Poor organization or inadequate facilities in other areas will impact on your audience and negate the effect of the main event.

Identify where other services such as registration, cloakroom and catering will be located in relation to the main event area and the entrances. Check the capacities and facilities of each of these areas against its purpose and the flow of traffic that will pass between them. As a guide, a registration area should be big enough for at least one registration table per 100 persons attending.

Seating

The size of your audience will obviously dictate the size of room you will require to hold your event. Most event venues can provide room plans that indicate the maximum capacities and various seating patterns. Seating styles will vary according to the nature of the event. Theatre style, banqueting, classroom or boardroom are most common but other configurations may meet your audience's needs better and can be discussed with the venue manager and/or technical services provider.

Catering

The venue manager should be able to advise you on the capacity of the catering area. If using an external catering company, ensure that they view the site to give their recommendations. It is always helpful if you can use a caterer who is familiar with the venue and has provided services there previously.

The dietary requirements of your audience should be checked. Ensure that special diets such as vegan, vegetarian, kosher, etc can be catered for.

Special needs

Members of your audience, or indeed presenters, may have special needs. For example, they may be wheelchair users or impaired visually or aurally. Obviously, it is not possible to cover every potential requirement for special needs here, but you should always take advice from organizations or individuals that represent such groups. However, the following are some of the most common special needs requirements:

■ induction loop for hearing aid users;
■ someone to 'sign' for the deaf;
■ use of subtitles with video.

For wheelchair users and the physically disabled:

■ ramped or level access to all areas, including the stage, clearly sign posted;
■ suitable parking and transport links;
■ doors should be lightweight or automatic and door widths should be checked;
■ corridors and entrance widths to be checked, particularly at tight corners or bends;
■ lifts should be able to accommodate the large type of electric wheelchair;
■ floor surfaces – avoid deep, heavy pile carpets that can hamper manoeuvrability. Hard floors should be slip proof, especially for stick or crutch users;
■ adequate number of suitable toilets;
■ catering area to allow for adequate access between tables;
■ if the event is residential, check that bedrooms are suitable for wheelchair users.

It is imperative that a suitable representative of the special needs group views the venue prior to booking in order to assess its suitability. Due to the scarcity of reasonably accessible venues in the United Kingdom there will inevitably be some compromise needed from time to time. Hopefully, this situation will improve since the Disability Discrimination Act became law in 1999.

Technical services

Most live events use some type of technical services in order to heighten the impact and effect of the message they wish to communicate. Whether this is just a flip chart and pens, or the latest video wall and computer graphics, you must always check whether these can be used in the venue you have chosen.

Size of audience and speakers' presentations usually dictate the amount and type of equipment you will require to help deliver your message. You may have some knowledge and experience of the type of technical equipment used but it is vital that you consult with your chosen technical services supplier or production company at a very early stage.

Screen/projection

Presentation can be either front or rear projected onto a screen surface. The advantage of rear projection is that no one can walk across the projector, creating a shadow and interrupting the flow of the presentation. Also, your presentation will appear much more professional with no cables or stands in the middle of the audience. The disadvantage is that more space is required in the presentation area to allow for the rear projection distance behind the screen. As a rough guide, allow for one-third of your room space to be behind the screen for back projection.

When using a presentation screen, the facility to black out the room is very important. Slides, computer graphics and overhead transparencies all use light to project the image onto the screen. If the room is not adequately blacked out, any ambient light will bleach the visuals out, making them impossible to view.

Ideally, you should have the facility to dim the room lights to a level that allows the screen images to be viewed whilst still keeping the presenter, who may be standing in front of the screen, visible. If your audience is large in number, the use of a lighting rig should be considered to spotlight the presenter's position and any other people on the stage.

Your technical services supplier or production company should advise you on a suitable screen size relative to the size of the venue, the number and positioning of your audience and any technical considerations. Also, the screen should be set at a height where all the audience can view it clearly. The size of the screen plus the head height of a seated audience (approximately four feet) will usually give the required minimum ceiling height of a presentation venue.

Stage

The larger your audience, the more important the use of a stage becomes. It will ensure that all of your audience can view the presenters. This is essential if your presenters will be seated at a table for a question and answer style debate. A stage or raised platform for speakers is normally recommended for an audience size over 75 delegates or for any size of audience where the speakers will be seated at a table.

Sound

An audience in excess of 75 delegates is also the size for which you should consider using a sound system to reinforce the presenters' speeches. The voice projection of speakers varies enormously so should not be relied on. The use of a good sound system is crucial because, at the risk of stating the obvious, if even part of your audience cannot hear what is being said the whole purpose of your event – communication – will be lost. Money spent on venue, hi-tech presentations, backdrops, etc will all be wasted if your presenter cannot be heard at the back of the room!

A professional sound system supplier should ask you the size of the audience and view the venue. Ensure that they know well in advance of any special needs such as induction loop facilities for hard of hearing delegates.

Speakers

Many technical facilities can be provided to help speakers communicate and interact with the audience. These include radio microphones, computer graphics, autocue, speakers' comfort monitors, laser pointers, satellite links, live camera relay of speakers onto a screen, video footage and delegate response handsets. These are not discussed here in detail because each speaker's requirements (and budgets) will vary. Liaise between your speakers and technical supplier to ascertain what is essential, desirable and affordable.

Stage set

When planning your event you should consider the use of a modular or custom-built stage set or backdrop. As well as creating a strong focal point for your audience, a set can help project a highly professional image of your organization and reinforce your communication objective through display of your organization's branding, sponsors' logos, conference slogan, etc. When choosing your venue, take account of the ceiling height, as this will be an important factor in the design of a stage set. The venue must be able to accommodate the height of the set or backdrop that will usually include a screen that will have to be set at a height to ensure it is clearly visible by all of the audience.

OTHER CONSIDERATIONS

Insurance

When using audiovisual equipment and stage sets on an event, your technical services supplier should provide event insurance with the equipment rental. This will cover them against public and legal liabilities in the unlikely case of accident or injury of delegates and speakers during the event. They should also provide equipment insurance in case of breakage or theft whilst on site and details should be obtained from the contractor to clarify the details.

Health and safety

It is essential that you always comply with current health and safety legislation when staging an event. The main areas to be aware of are: do not exceed the audience capacity of the venue; do not obstruct the fire exits; and do not use electrical equipment that has not been safety-tested. The responsibility for equipment testing will normally fall on the supplier.

Venue-finding agencies

You can undertake a venue search yourself. However, a cost and time effective way to find a venue that suits all your requirements would be to use the services of a venue-finding agency. They operate in a similar way to a travel agent and, as well as taking out much of the 'leg work' of the task, can negotiate preferential rates for you using their buying power.

Most county councils or tourist boards now have their own agencies set up to find venues in their area. Alternatively, a list of commercial agencies can be obtained from the Meetings Industry Association based in Worcester. Commercial agencies have knowledge of national and international venues as well as local venues. If using a venue-finding agency you should brief them as fully as possible, including details of your objectives, audience, methods of communication and budgets in order that they may find a venue that suits your exact needs. Once you obtain a list of possible venues, a site visit is always recommended.

Legal/contractual considerations

When booking a venue or services for an event you should always be aware of the contractual obligations you are entering into. The most commonly enforced contractual clause is the venue cancellation charge. Nearly all venues will enforce a charge in the event of cancellation. This can be up to 95 per cent of the contract value depending on how close to the booking date you cancel the event. This should be borne in mind when booking a venue for an event that will rely on ticket sales to cover the costs of the venue.

Delegate management

The logistics involved in ensuring your audience arrives trouble-free to your event is always more time consuming than you imagine. Invitations, booking forms, response handling and joining instructions are only the beginning of the pre-event administration process. Accommodation allocation, seating plans, badges, conference folders and presentation handouts will then be required on site. Always plan carefully the administration you will require and allow plenty of time.

SCOPE CONFERENCE

The following case study illustrates many of the production and technical issues to be addressed when planning a live event. Whilst this example is for a relatively large-scale event, most of the issues dealt with also apply for a very small-scale event.

Objectives:	To communicate the charity's successes in the past. To set aims and objectives for the future. To launch the Accessibility Exhibition. To highlight current campaign/policy initiative.
Audience:	500 delegates, many with physical disabilities.
Theme/Style:	Utilize the Scope corporate image/colours whilst highlighting the campaign/policy initiative. Provide a launch vehicle for the Accessibility Exhibition.

Venue: Marquee at the rear of the Norbreck Castle Hotel, Blackpool. This venue was selected because of the relatively high number of wheelchair converted bedrooms as well as satisfying the event requirements for audience size and good wheelchair access. The conference was held in the marquee (which was there by chance from a previous event and hence very cost effective), whilst the exhibition was held in the hotel exhibition hall.

Special Considerations: High number of stick and wheelchair user delegates/speakers.
Deaf and hard of hearing delegates.
Vegetarian dietary requirements.

Execution: The venue was assessed for wheelchair users and found to be satisfactory. A signer was provided for deaf delegates and an induction loop for the hearing aid wearers. The conference stage had a ramp added to allow wheelchair speakers access to the raised platform. Regulation ramp incline 1m high–12m long.

Audience: Approximately 500 delegates in theatre-style presentation.

Technical Services: The conference made use of a rear projection screen with computer presentations and live camera relay.
A sound system was required with a fully controllable lighting rig.

Execution: The marquee had to be assessed to see if it could accommodate 500 people seated in a theatre-style arrangement with enough room for an extra large aisle for wheelchair users to manoeuvre easily. In addition, space was required for a stage, backdrop and screen with space behind for rear projection. The blackout level was also of an adequate standard to view the screen presentation clearly.

Scope used a basic, but effective, custom-built stage set that was finished in the organization's corporate colours and logo. The event sponsor's logo was also incorporated into the design. The overall effect was a professional image presented to an audience of delegates and media representatives.

Summary: Organizing a successful event is no secret; all it takes is good preparation. Each task should follow a critical path with deadlines set when important decisions have to be made. Good planning will make an event organizer's job so much easier and hopefully good fun.

You need not always organize your own event. It is possible to use events as a marketing tool through taking part in those organized by other organizations.

These could be fringe meetings, presentations or stalls in an exhibition area. If you are planning to have a stall at an external event, there are some key points to bear in mind:

■ Find out as much as you can about the audience at the event before booking and planning an exhibition stall. On average, staffing a stall effectively will need at least four persons working in shifts throughout a day.
■ Base your stall design and your decisions about literature and staffing on the nature of the audience. If it is a specialist social services conference, you will need to be able to answer technical questions. If it is a youth event, young people on your stall are essential.

■ Try not to bombard people with literature. Have two or three key things you want to communicate and use the literature to support them.
■ Try to find a way of engaging people in conversation. Petitions are an excellent way of making an initial approach to passers-by. Think carefully, however, about whether or not to have give-aways such as pens, mouse mats, sweets, etc.
■ Draw up a stall rota and stick to it. There is nothing more off-putting to visitors than a gaggle of staff or volunteers gossiping behind and in front of the stand while using the literature space as a resting place for coffee cups.

YOUR OWN EXHIBITIONS

Many smaller charities have open days or other events at which they organize mini exhibitions. These can be an excellent way of informing or updating key audiences about what you do and can help engage staff from across the organization.

■ Make a list of the separate stalls or exhibition spaces you will have at the event. Add in any speaker sessions.
■ Make a list of what these will be called.
■ Then stop and think about who is likely to come to the event. Put yourself in the position of one of your potential visitors and think about the questions he or she is likely to ask and the information he or she is seeking.
■ Mentally 'walk through' how he or she will go about this. Will he or she immediately understand the titles being used; will he or she need to visit several stands to get the answer to seemingly simple questions?
■ If your visitor's visit has become seemingly complex, you will need to rename or reorganize some parts of the event, or consider a 'one stop shop' stall for complicated questions. Design the day so that people do not need to be passed from person to person too much.
■ Think carefully before naming sessions or displays after departments in your organization. If the activities of the department are 100 per cent obvious from the name, then you have no problem. Departmental names in charities, however, often

mean little to people not in the know. What does 'support services' mean, for example?

■ Consider organizing stalls and events by 'market'. You could consider grouping cross-departmental activities under a title related to the relevant beneficiary – 'Services for children', 'Information and advice for teachers', 'How to get involved with the charity'.

■ Plan for a number of staff or helpers with no particular responsibility. They should be available to give directions, to answer simple questions and to make introductions.

■ Ensure everyone logs queries whether answered immediately or not. Make a commitment to send follow-up material, or answer very complicated questions by mail. This helps ensure that names, addresses and areas of interest are recorded and that you can cross-promote related services or activities.

10

Annual reports as marketing tools

Veronica Crichton

Too many charity annual reports are boring and a waste of time for all except those who make a living producing them. Yet, an annual report will often be the only publication in which money is invested and that is intended to sum up the importance of the organization for a wide range of readers. That many charities get this wrong is a clear example of a marketing opportunity lost.

In this chapter, 'annual report' refers to more than the statutory tables of accounts and reporting notes. In some charities, this is called the annual review. Whichever word is used, this chapter is about the annual publication that serves as a brochure about what the charity has done and, if produced properly, communicates a sense of what the charity will do. So why do these publications often fail?

Much of the reason lies in process. Annual reports are usually spawned by committee and delivered through an interminable schedule of meetings. They are hampered by a lack of strategic vision and hamstrung by that language peculiar to the voluntary sector which, in the opinion of some cynics, seems to work on the principle that if no one can understand what you are saying, no one can blame you.

In some reports an aura of self-congratulation creeps in, with every department demanding 'our page' so that the world may know how successfully the human resources team has filled eight vacancies and organized a splendid send-off for dear old Cynthia after her 20 hard years on the job. This is all a great shame.

Annual reports are a heavy drain on budgets. They are also a great opportunity to sell the organization to a key audience. But this will not happen just because a committee passes a resolution that it should. Strategic thought and discipline are needed.

Whatever the finance department say, and it will probably be said with ever-increasing emphasis, the statutory bits of the annual report can be presented simply in diagrams towards the end of the document. The rest is whatever you want to make of it.

The annual report is a key communications tool and should be treated as such. It needs to be well thought out, well written, well presented and fine tuned to appeal to an identified audience.

Having overseen a number of annual reports, I find that when asked, 'What is your report for?' most organizations reply something like, 'Fundraising and to persuade people to buy our services... I think it's nice if the staff get a mention... We need to show the trustees what we're doing... and of course the service users just love it... of course, it's all for them.'

To the next question, which is, 'How are you going to achieve this?', the answer is equally clear-cut: 'I want everyone to feel a sense of shared ownership of the report.' Or from those who have mastered the post-1997 phrases, 'I want it to be inclusive – full of joined-up thinking so everyone can sign up to it.' Such statements are probably sincere, they may be laudable, but they do not make for good publications.

Too many people in the charitable world do not take the trouble to sit down and work out what a publication can do for them, and what it cannot do. Humpty Dumpty said that a word meant whatever he chose it to mean. But in today's highly competitive world, thought transference is not an option.

Before producing any publication, but especially before producing the annual report, the organization must establish:

■ who the audience is;
■ what the message is;
■ how that message can be got across.

Keen thought needs to be given at an early stage about how the audience is going to consume the report. Will it be one of many that pass their desks? Why should they read it thoroughly? Readers will not be students facing an exam on your inner working. On the whole, they are not swatting up for a job interview. They are not filling in a bid application based on the vital information in your report. They may not know your world. They almost certainly would not speak your language.

If they are worth targeting, they are probably important. That means they are probably busy people. Your report has to grab their attention, and hold it for a reasonable time. In this context, 'reasonable' means three to five minutes. The publication needs to tell them what you want them to know, and to show them in a way they can absorb quickly. This means a clear vision and a clear message. It means sticking to your message and not letting every member of the senior management team add in their tuppence worth. It needs to be written in jargon-free language that an intelligent 12 year old could understand. It needs to be packed full of examples. It needs to be an easy read.

No one is paid to read your annual report. You have to make them want to do so. The purpose of the report is to impress the target audiences with your excellence, proficiency or suitability to do the job. The publication will only achieve this if the recipient can absorb the message while dialling a telephone number. That is the window of opportunity.

In the field of mass communication, more is less. More information means less comprehension. I have seen many annual reports that could bore for Britain! It is better to tell the audience one interesting fact well rather than give them so much that they put the report to one side for 'later'.

Common weaknesses:

▧ bad pictures, usually with no people in them and taken by someone 'keen on taking pictures';
▧ pictures scattered through the publication the size of postage stamps – this is not good design, merely poor use of photography;
▧ dense wedges of text across the whole width of the page;
▧ language that means nothing to the audience (what are 'special needs', what is the support services department?);

▓ internally focused messages that concentrate on your processes rather than the difference you make for the people who rely on your services.

Planning is vital at every stage. The message of the annual report starts from the moment it emerges from the envelope or appears in the in tray. Decisions like the number of pages, the quality of the paper and the use of colour are all part of the message. It must look professional, but you should also decide whether an expensive feel is the right image for your organization. The suggestion that a fortune has been spent on the publication is counter-productive.

A STEP-BY-STEP GUIDE – THINKING AND PLANNING

▓ Put one person in charge of editing or coordinating the annual report. This person must have the full backing of the chief executive and be senior and tough enough to withstand complaints and lobbying from heads of departments.
▓ Have a clear view of who the audience is.
▓ Know what you want to communicate. Two key messages will be sufficient.
▓ Think about the 'how' of communication and establish a style. Choices include third-person text, first-person stories, messages from the great and good, rhyming couplets, blank verse, etc.
▓ Agree a consistent approach to words. It does not matter whether you use capital or lower-case letters for job titles. It does matter if you are inconsistent.
▓ Think about the type of pictures you need and get them. Do not rely on whatever is in the cupboard.
▓ Think about the number of pages you need and about where the page breaks will be.
▓ Think about when it needs to be distributed and work backwards. If you are inexperienced, give yourself a good three months' lead time.

STEP-BY-STEP GUIDE – DOING IT

■ Once you have decided the photographs you need, commission a professional to do the work. You will need big, bold pictures. These are what draw readers' eyes to a page and make them want to read the text. Good pictures can also be used for other purposes such as exhibitions, slide presentations, Web sites, the local media and so on. It is, in fact, a good idea to use the pictures elsewhere. You are establishing a look and a style for the organization through the publication, and the repetition of key images will help. If you do not know a photographer, it is worth asking your local council press office, or the local newspaper, for names of those who will take on freelance work.

■ Establish ways of getting and recording permission to use photographs. A wonderful front cover will come back to haunt you if you did not have permission to photograph that child whose parents decide to complain loudly.

■ Commission a designer and agree a format. You will need to decide how this publication fits with your corporate image. If you do not have a corporate image, the publication may help establish one. Corporate images stick in the public mind through repetition, so try to stick to yours. *Kit Kat* and *Coca-Cola* do not change their colours or logo each year just to stop staff getting bored. As a general rule of thumb, if you are beginning to be bored with the image, the audience is only just catching on to it. If you do not know any designers, your local council's PR department may be able to suggest some. If you see a publication you particularly like, it is worth asking who designed it, and who printed it. Other charities are usually very happy to help with this information.

■ Establish how you will be billed with your designer. Will it be by the project or by the hours worked? Agree a ballpark price but be aware that there are likely to be changes. Communicate clearly to colleagues that author's corrections may well increase the price quoted.

■ Establish who needs to check text and get them to agree to check at manuscript stage before design work is done. Changes done on your own computer cost nothing but your time. Establish also whether you are asking people to check for accuracy or for style. Asking non-writers to check for style is usually a mistake.

■ Establish who will write the copy. Then stick to your decision.

MORE ABOUT COPY WRITING

Writing the copy is probably one of the most vexed aspects of report production. As a copywriter with more than 20 years' experience, I am constantly amazed at how people will pay high prices for print and design and then write the most terrible copy themselves.

Most copywriters would admit to having no idea of how to run a charity. Unfortunately, most people who work in the voluntary sector think they can write. For those not used to the process of editorial production, including being edited, having their copy changed is an emotional invasion of traumatic proportions. Added to the problem of dealing with this is that every senior member of the organization will want to rewrite the text. This needs to be resisted.

Unless you are lucky enough to have someone in-house who can write simple, direct English, it is worth hiring a professional writer. It is then his or her job to convert information for the wider audience. Some charities hesitate to hire professionals because 'they won't understand the organization'. But not initially understanding the organization is a benefit in this context. The writer needs to start from the perspective of the audience, which also, by definition, does not have the same level of understanding as staff and trustees.

It is important to agree a ballpark price with your writer before you start. Experienced writers working with a new client are likely to put a cautionary clause in the contract in case you are the type of organization where everyone has a rewrite or where copy is changed after approval. It is important that this is communicated to colleagues likely to want last-minute changes.

THE PRODUCTION PROCESS

I am often asked whether design or copy comes first. As mentioned earlier, the ideas must come first, but it really does not matter whether you produce text before design or design before text. I have found in the past that it saves time and money to write the copy after the rough designs are done. That way I can write to a precise word count knowing I will not have to cut or expand later.

The print process is where a lot of money can go missing. When you seek quotes from your printer, draw up a specification of what you want. This should include information about page size, paper weight, cover details, colours and processes to be used, number of copies, delivery address and deadlines and so on. If you are not sure what to specify, your designer or copywriter should be able to help you. Make sure you obtain three quotes to establish an idea of the likely cost.

Deciding on quantity can be a problem. On the one hand, you want enough to go round. On the other hand, boxes of undistributed annual reports are a waste of money and a storage problem. If you have no previous records, look at your mailing lists, membership figures and so on and come up with an estimate.

There are a number of options for colour. You could print in one colour – remember black is a colour. You could choose one main colour and one 'spot' colour. You could use two colours, neither of which is black. You could use black and two colours, or you could use full colour printing. You can also give the appearance of more colour by using black and white photography with one extra colour in a duotone effect. Such choices depend on price and message. Remember that less is more – the simple choice can often have a clearer effect.

If you do choose full colour, you will want to see what is called a 'wet proof' or 'Chromalin'. This is a full colour printer's proof and is produced so that you can check colours are as you want them and that the pictures will reproduce correctly. The proof can cost you hundreds of pounds, so there is no point in having it if you do not leave yourself enough time to put mistakes right. Make sure you build thinking and checking time into the production process.

Your designer may offer to handle print buying for you. Print and paper quality is of great importance to designers so this should mean that quality is assured. Think carefully, however, because many designers put mark-ups on their print buying, so the saving in time may not be worth the money.

It is worth spending time getting to know a few good printers.

Many will happily show you round their plant and explain some of the technical terms you are likely to come across.

KEY POINTS THAT ARE OFTEN FORGOTTEN

■ This may sound obvious, but the cover is what people will see first. This includes the back cover. Make sure the design conveys your key message and that the back is attractive. You cannot be sure which side of the report will come out of the envelope first. Furthermore, publications displayed on racks or tables can end up the wrong way round, and if your outside back cover is a boring list of trustees, it will not be picked up.

■ If you are mailing the report, the outside cover will be handled by whomever stuffs the envelopes, so make sure it is finger-print proof.

■ Make sure your name and logo are clearly identifiable on the front. All too frequently, logos appear without a name.

■ Your charity number must be on the publication. Under the address on the back cover is an obvious place.

■ Make sure your address, telephone, fax and e-mail numbers are easy to find and read. The job of the annual report is to stimulate interest. This means it must be easy for people to contact you. Response mechanisms, like tear-off forms, can work too.

■ Think carefully about the message from the chairman (or patron). Does this really need to be the first thing people see? The answer may be yes, but do not assume. There is no rule saying that the great and good come before client stories.

■ Make sure the graphics about finances are easy to understand. Your finance director has already read the balance sheet. The finance section in the report is for people who are not about to read all the details.

■ Think carefully about long lists of any kind. Do you really need lists of members of staff or trustees? Is there a more interesting way of presenting lists of fund givers?

■ Picture captions and headlines can be difficult to write. Leave time to get them right.

■ Look at the opportunities of the centre spread. There are many ways of using this creatively and it is worth spending some time over it.

▓ Get the mailing list right. There is no point in spending time and money on a professional publication and then annoying key people by double and triple mailing them. Double check circulation lists and think about distribution at the same time as you think about production.

11

Evaluation tools and techniques

Mark Westaby and Peter Crowe

For anybody involved in the evaluation industry, the temptation to fill a chapter entitled *Evaluation tools and techniques* with detailed statistics, graphs and charts is enormous. Yet, we have resisted this temptation for good reasons.

To do the subject justice in a single chapter is impossible. There are a number of other sources that cover such detail for anybody who wishes to take the time to research this further. Also, much evaluation is not rocket science nor is it easy to do properly, and it is certainly not a trivial undertaking. We would therefore encourage those who think it would be simple to read a chapter of a book and develop their own evaluation system to think again. It is, without doubt, much cheaper and more effective to call in the experts to do it for you!

Evaluation has come a long way over the past decade, with new techniques being introduced to meet the needs of increasingly sophisticated marketing programmes. For instance, media analysis is now an industry in its own right and is successfully addressing the needs of the PR industry in measuring media relations programmes, yet it was rarely used at the start of the 1990s.

Despite these developments, many UK organizations in both the charity and commercial sectors continue to invest heavily in marketing programmes with no clear idea of the objectives they seek to achieve. Too little attention continues to be paid by organizations of all types and sizes to the critical need for an integrated approach in achieving accountability.

Fortunately, this is changing. A trend is developing towards more and better use of integrated evaluation, planning and research across the marketing industries. Much of the reason for this has been the different levels of sophistication needed by the various marketing disciplines. While sophisticated methods have been used to support some marketing disciplines, most notably advertising, precious little has been done to develop and integrate this with other key areas such as public relations.

This has not been a major problem in the past, as the world's media remained largely unchanged for many years. Apart from a few minor exceptions, the marketing professional's role in communicating with target audiences could be planned using traditional methods or even, in the case of PR, on an intuitive basis. For instance, charities wishing to reach a defined readership could do so by breaking the national newspapers into broadsheets and tabloids, with a further simple breakdown of the latter depending on the demographics required. Broadly speaking, the same has been true for television and radio. Beyond the national media, it has also been relatively simple to plan campaigns regionally and by special interest. Over the years, the media have started to change. Satellite and cable television have expanded the viewers' choice beyond traditional terrestrial alternatives; and radio has been deregulated, with vastly more local and specialist channels available.

Now, even more change is occurring. If the past 50 years have been relatively stable, the next 5 to 10 will see more change than has been experienced since the Industrial Revolution. Indeed, some industry commentators believe that what is happening is more akin to the invention of the printing press, which has probably been the most profound development to affect society over the past millennium.

The reason for this change is two-fold. First, the Internet and World Wide Web; and second, the advent of digital media. As a result of these developments, traditional media planning rules will fly out of the window. Instead of reaching mass audiences through a few media, the choice available to readers, listeners and viewers will mean that they will have to be reached through a much larger number of fragmented communication channels.

Audiences will have more and more choice as to where they can source ever-increasing amounts of information. As a result, competition for people's attention will inevitably increase. The organizations that gain maximum attention from key audiences will be those that provide the most absorbing, useful and appropriate information to the right people at the right time. Traditional planning rules will no longer apply and the marketing industries must adapt accordingly.

In an increasingly competitive world, good planning and evaluation are essential to maximize results from marketing programmes and to reduce the large amount of time and resources wasted in targeting the wrong audiences. Good planning means defining clear objectives for marketing programmes at all levels, which can then be used as the benchmark against which the evaluation process can be carried out. While such objectives should be driven from the centre to ensure consistency and maximize resources, it is important to take account of an organization's overall requirements and to recognize that some degree of flexibility is important, particularly where regional activities are concerned.

A good, if obvious, example can be taken from the Royal National Lifeboat Institution. While the overall objectives for the RNLI remain consistent, it hardly needs a planning or measurement guru to recognize that awareness and appreciation of this tremendous organization is heightened by the proximity of any member of the target audience to the sea. As a result, being reminded of the dangers involved simply to get a meal onto the table of a fish and chip restaurant in Leeds can require quite different techniques to those needed when visiting Scarborough and being invited to dip our hands into our pockets for our incredibly brave lifeboatmen. The marketing objectives must reflect this difference.

Every penny of budget must be spent carefully and with the knowledge that it will gain maximum return on investment. Thus, the need for carefully planned and thoroughly evaluated marketing programmes has never been greater and this is as important in the charity sector as in the commercial world. Indeed, some argue that it is even more so.

These are simple points but it never ceases to amaze how frequently marketing programmes are carried out merely 'because they are a good idea'. Good ideas are important. But they are not enough without a proper assessment of the benefits that will be achieved and a careful definition of exactly how success will be measured. In order to achieve this, charity organizations should note the following list of points.

1. Establish at the outset the 'business' goals that need to be achieved. While charities are non-profit making, they are nonetheless business-orientated organizations that must survive in an increasingly competitive world. Where possible, these business goals should be measurable, in which case they become objectives in the strict sense of the word.
2. Define the marketing communication goals needed to achieve the business goals, as well as the messages that will need to be delivered, keeping these as simple and succinct as possible. Also, identify the target audiences that need to be reached, not only in terms of the sectors that need to be addressed but also the management levels of decision makers and influencers who need to be targeted.
3. Do NOT heave a big sigh of relief and stop the planning process here. This is the start point, not the end!
4. Having established marketing communication goals, messages and audiences, the next step is to prioritize them. The reason for this is simple – and important. Unless prioritized, how will you and, most importantly, the rest of the marketing team know where they should be putting most of what are always valuable resources? By prioritizing at the planning stage, you will avoid wasting valuable resources that will be better utilized elsewhere.
5. Involve as many people as is practically possible in defining the goals, messages and audiences in order to gain maximum 'buy in'. These people should not only consist of people from the rest of the organization, which the marketing programmes should be supporting (if not, then why not?), but also representatives from all marketing communication disciplines, such as advertising, direct marketing and PR. This will ensure

maximum integration of marketing programmes at the planning stage.

6. Having established prioritized goals, messages and audiences, these should now be used as a template against which resources can be allocated and detailed activities defined.
7. Define a timetable of activity, which should include advertising and PR media plans, direct marketing activity, etc. A PR-related media relations programme should have a media plan just as an advertising campaign should have a media plan. This should be determined against audiences defined, both in sectors to be reached and management levels targeted.
8. Integrate all marketing communication activities.
9. Establish measurement criteria at the outset and planning stage. These should be easy to understand and clearly communicated to everybody involved in the marketing programme, both inside and outside the organization.
10. Successful planning requires accurate feedback. Ensure that measurement programmes are properly budgeted and that results are fed back into programmes, which can be fine-tuned or redirected as appropriate. Remember, if you cannot measure it, you cannot control it.

In a world of rapid change, it is essential that organizations review their business objectives on a regular basis. Otherwise, it is difficult to see how marketing programmes can be planned and implemented to take proper account of such rapidly changing market conditions.

One question often asked is just how much should be spent on evaluation. This will depend to some extent on the marketing programme in question. For instance, the general rule of thumb for the PR industry is that ten per cent of an annual PR budget should be spent on measurement, depending on the overall size of the budget. If the budget is significant, then a smaller proportion should be quite adequate. Ultimately, it is a matter of judgement, which of course depends on for what the evaluation is being used. For instance, consider a charity seeking a significant new sponsorship deal or looking to justify an existing one. Such a charity would do well to invest significantly in evaluation, which can be used to prove conclusively the benefits it has to offer.

However, there is no disguising that this can be a particularly difficult question for those charities with small PR budgets. While media analysis, for instance, does not have to be expensive, anything spent on evaluation for these organizations is bound to take away a significant proportion of what little PR budget is available. As with all difficult questions, there are no easy answers, but it is always worth exploring the possibilities. One of Metrica's non-profit sector clients is the British Bobsleigh Association. This organization uses media analysis most effectively as a means to prove to sponsors its ability to generate coverage in key media, despite a shoestring budget of just a few hundred pounds.

Even organizations with little or no budget for external evaluation can and should still apply the basic principles set out above. By setting clear, measurable objectives at the outset of a PR programme, they at least have a sound benchmark against which to assess just how well they have done.

At this point, it is also worth considering what organizations should NOT be tempted to do, with or without a budget for evaluation. Again, the PR industry provides an excellent example of what does NOT constitute good practice, in the guise of the 'advertising value equivalent', or AVE. The use of AVEs has generated considerable debate within the PR industry. In Metrica's view – and indeed this is now accepted across the PR industry – AVEs are worthless. It is worth reiterating some of the reasons why this is the case:

■ Editorial is not and never will be 'free advertising'. Editorial and advertising complement each other but should never be compared in the way they are under AVEs.
■ The basic data on which AVEs are determined is impossible to define. How, for instance, is BBC airtime valued? Even those media that do accept advertising have wildly varying rates, which can change on the strength of a telephone call. Not much of a standard there.
■ How do AVEs take account of 'favourability'? There is no such thing as 'negative advertising' and it is nonsense to suggest otherwise.
■ AVEs generate large numbers, which are often used by PR professionals to demonstrate the 'value' of coverage achieved. In fact, they tell the client nothing about the target audiences that have been reached and can be very misleading.

One of the major reasons for using AVEs, often quoted by their supporters, is that there are no credible alternatives. Yet, this is simply not the case. One solution, which Metrica uses with great success, is to analyse targets reached through audience figures that are available and can be compared for many media, including the BBC. Such figures will never be 100 per cent perfect, but they are properly researched and infinitely more credible and useful than AVEs, which should be consigned to the scrap heap.

Many PR professionals believe that press coverage is 'free advertising'. While it is not difficult to understand why such a belief has developed, the PR industry must stop making comparisons between advertising and editorial coverage if PR is to continue to gain respect as a strategic management tool. Both are complex, powerful forms of communication, but they work in completely different ways.

Market research is another valuable tool both for planning and evaluating campaigns. Again, it is almost inevitable that the response from many charities is: 'We don't have the budget!' Consider the following two points:

■ Properly designed research does not need to be expensive. In the two case studies detailed here (RNLI and John Grooms), research was carried out within a tight budget.
■ Research works. If your past experience of market research is that you briefly look through the report and then put it on the shelf, then something is wrong. Either the brief was wrong or the research was wrong – and a good research company will advise you on altering your brief to produce cost-effective research.

As already outlined, the whole point of planning is to ensure that your activity has the best chance of success when it actually takes place. Research can help by:

■ providing insights into the current situation in the 'market place';
■ identifying the target audiences who are most likely to respond;
■ identifying the messages that are most likely to work;
■ aiding media/communications channel planning;
■ testing activity ideas before they 'go live'.

Again, this process does not need to be expensive. A little bit of digging can reveal a treasure trove of existing information. Also, one piece of research can cover a number of these areas. Useful techniques are 'quantitative' and 'qualitative' research.

Quantitative research – a survey of, say, 400 people in your target audience can provide invaluable information about awareness of and attitudes towards your organization. This can perform a number of functions. It helps you to answer the question 'Where are we now?' and, therefore, aids you in setting your objectives and strategies. It also provides benchmarks against which the success of your activity can be judged. Furthermore, suitable questions can provide content for press releases during the campaign.

Qualitative research – a small number of focus groups or even one-to-one interviews can be very useful in helping organizations to understand how their publics view them. They enable you to 'get beneath the skin' and understand what people really think and, perhaps more importantly, feel. They are also useful for 'pre-testing' campaign ideas. It is surprising how many marketing ideas have come completely from insights gained in focus groups.

The real question about market research is not 'Can we afford to do it?' so much as 'Can we afford not to do it?' If you do not understand your target audience, how can you be sure that your campaign will work?

THE ROYAL NATIONAL LIFEBOAT INSTITUTION

During 1999, the RNLI celebrated its 175th anniversary. A large number of events were planned around the country, and in particular, a road show would tour the country describing the history of the RNLI and promoting its present-day work. The Institution approached Metrica Research with a brief to:

▓ evaluate the success of the road show;
▓ track its effect on awareness of and attitudes towards the RNLI;
▓ evaluate the success of the various sections of the road show;
▓ measure awareness of other events organized for the anniversary year;
▓ measure awareness of the RNLI's *Safety on the Sea* campaign.

The RNLI was particularly concerned about its image among young people, and perception of its relevance to the modern age. Metrica designed a research programme in which a sample of people would be interviewed before entering the road show and another group would be interviewed after attending it. This way the effect of the exhibits on awareness and attitudes could be monitored. In addition, the sample was deliberately biased towards younger people.

Before seeing the road show, 232 interviews were conducted, and 243 after. Although there was a consistently high awareness of the organization, there were significant improvements in both knowledge of the RNLI and attitudes towards it, particularly with regard to its modernity and efficiency. The number of people agreeing that it was a modern and efficient service rose from 88 per cent to 97 per cent.

The survey also provided significant information on the relative popularity of different sections of the road show, awareness of other anniversary events and the 'Safety on the Sea' campaign. While the RNLI can congratulate itself that the road show was a success, it has also gained valuable information for future planning in a number of areas.

JOHN GROOMS

John Grooms is a charity providing a number of services for disabled people including housing, care services and holidays. It is also involved in campaigning for more positive attitudes towards disabled people, particularly in the workplace. It had run advertising campaigns on London Underground but had never done any kind of evaluation. Metrica was approached with a view to evaluating their campaign on escalator advertisements.

A quantitative approach was recommended under which 200 persons would be interviewed before the campaign broke, split between two stations – one in the West End and one in the City. It was important that research was carried out throughout the day between 8.00 am and 6.00 pm. The sample was designed to match London Underground users by age and sex.

Respondents were asked whether they agreed with a number of

statements about what disabled people could do – my job, become a model, pass GCSEs, etc, as well as statements like 'disabled people can do anything that they want', or 'disabled people are just as capable of getting on in the workplace as able-bodied people'. These questions were carefully designed to ensure that people did not just say the 'right thing'.

The questionnaire also looked at prompted and unprompted awareness of John Grooms and other charities, as well as people's views about what John Grooms does. The second phase – at the same stations with the same samples – will ask the same awareness and attitude questions, but also look at prompted and unprompted awareness of the advertising and its success at communicating some of the charity's key messages.

The results of the survey will be helpful in providing evaluation of the tube advertising and answering questions as to whether it is working or how it could be improved. It will also provide general information about awareness of John Grooms and attitudes towards disabled people.

12

Integrated campaigning

Neil Churchill

Integration is like innovation. It gets paid a lot of lip service but can often be misunderstood or taken for granted. Quite often, integration can be mistaken for internal communication, which is tantamount to viewing it through the wrong end of a telescope. Rather, integrated marketing communications has been defined as 'the careful co-ordination of multiple communication channels to deliver a clear, consistent and compelling message about an organization' (Kotler *et al*, 1999).

Integration does not start with a good idea, which is then spread across an organization. It should be a planned process that unifies different functions and tools behind common goals. Of course, good ideas are essential but they should be a product of good strategy, rather than a substitute for it.

In 1995, I worked for a large national charity that employed a marketing agency and an advertising consultancy, each managed by different departments. Pulling together a unified strategy often seemed the most challenging aspect of integration! Today, most of those same charities have restructured their in-house teams and rationalized their use of agencies as the old distinctions between above and below-the-line activity have been replaced by a more holistic approach to marketing. The results have been witnessed to notable effect in a number of high-profile campaigns run by organizations such as the NSPCC, who now seem to be competing on a level with commercial entities.

This book, however, is not aimed only at employees of the NSPCC. Rather, it assumes that most organizations do not have the brand equity, the in-house expertise or the finances to take the same approach to integrated marketing. But although few can hope to imitate the mega brands, there are nevertheless some important lessons to be learned by small and medium-sized organizations about the value of integrated campaigns. These can be summarized thus: integrate to maximize impact – fail to integrate and dissipate the value of even the very best ideas.

Integration has three core benefits:

1. Marketing campaigns often pursue multiple goals. They can seek to raise awareness, generate funds, build the brand and motivate stakeholders. Integration is therefore critical if organizations are to avoid sending mixed messages or advancing one objective at the expense of the others.
2. Most not-for-profit organizations work with limited budgets. However, there is still a temptation to view marketing activity from a functional perspective, with media relations following one course and direct marketing another. Integration is vital in order to achieve maximum impact on target audiences with limited funds. Communications need to prepare the ground for fundraising and fundraising needs to reinforce the messages of communications. These should not work against each other.
3. External campaigns can have a tremendous motivational and unifying impact on staff, volunteers and donors. But ownership requires understanding and commitment, which can only come through integration.

If integrated campaigns are so successful, why then are they so hard to achieve in practice? This chapter sets out the main ingredients for a successful integrated campaign and identifies ways to overcome some of the most common barriers to integration. It illustrates these techniques with examples from small and medium-sized organizations that have often developed effective campaigns without the benefit of strategic advice from marketing agencies.

WHAT DO WE MEAN BY INTEGRATION?

Integration is a planned process for developing and managing a campaign, whatever the goals of that campaign might be. A useful checklist has been devised which can be adapted for the not-for-profit sector (Smith, Bery and Pulford, 1999).

1. **Vertical integration.** It seems obvious to say that marketing campaigns should be consistent with the corporate goals, values and strategies of your organization. In practice, however, this is not always so simple. Sometimes a campaign can actually be seen to undermine the values of the organization. This might occur if a charity were to accept sponsorship from a company whose activities were perceived to conflict with the charity's aims. The Red Cross' association with Nestlé, for example, was criticized by some supporters because the company's distribution of baby milk powder in the developing world seemed to conflict with the charity's advocacy of breast-feeding (Wall, 2000). This is also a live issue in the environmental movement, where a division has opened up over corporate sponsorship between campaigners, who fear compromise, and pragmatists, who argue for influence from within.

2. **Horizontal integration.** Organizations must also be careful to ensure that campaigns are consistent with the activities of other departments, including human resources, and are consistent with investment policies or individual service strategies. This is especially important at a time when charities are increasingly being questioned and scrutinized by their stakeholders and the media.

   One danger is that charities are not always seen to practise what they preach. There is a fundamental inconsistency between launching a fundraising drive at a time when reserves stand at record levels, or in criticizing statutory provision when the organization's own services are highly restrictive or considered to be of poor quality. This problem may be especially acute for organizations working with disadvantaged client groups, who may find they are discriminating further in their own recruitment or volunteering policies. In these cases, all it would take would be one case of apparent injustice for an organization to be accused of double standards. It may not be easy to challenge ineffective policies. However, your level of confidence in these corporate procedures can certainly influence your choice of campaign theme.

3. **Marketing mix.** It is generally accepted that the famous 'Four P's' of marketing are more suited to consumer goods than to the not-for-profit sector. However, Bruce has argued for the use of 'Eight P's' in the voluntary sector (Bruce, 1998). These criteria can help marketing teams ensure that integration is considered from several important perspectives:

   – **Product.** In practice, the 'product' could be a fundraising proposition, a campaign goal, a powerful idea for change or even a package of benefits like a friends scheme. This product needs to be carefully designed to meet the needs of consumers, rather than internal or historical needs. If research suggests that a product no longer works, the charity should try to design one that does. This means accepting that products are not sacrosanct.

   – **Price.** Although this seems less relevant in the not-for-profit sector, it is actually vital. The price you attach to a major donor campaign can help determine the perceived value of the service you are hoping to establish. Similarly, Bruce argues that charities must consider the cost of their operations in terms of ratios of administration to direct charitable spend. This can be a hugely significant factor.

   – **Place.** Your campaign may be perceived differently depending on your choice of media (eg inserts versus door drops) or channels (eg a high-street store versus the local community centre). Campaigns on behalf of disadvantaged groups can be undermined if materials appear too glossy. Many charities are trying to find innovative ways of grabbing attention without appearing to waste money. Shelter mailed its warm supporters using a stamp to make the envelope look more personal. Small touches like this can often make a big difference.

   – **Promotion.** Most creative energy goes into the development of promotional activity and the earlier chapters in this book cover a number of different tools that can be used. However, it is vital to ensure that promotions contain substance as well as style. There is often a temptation to pursue good ideas that would not help advance the overall goal or message. In the early 1990s, the National Children's Home re-launched itself as NCH Action for Children using research that made a direct comparison between the Victorian era and modern times. Arguably, this was not a good way to demonstrate the charity's place in the modern world.

- **Physical evidence.** Charities are often judged by the standard of their premises. At Crisis during the build up to Christmas, the accumulation of donations in crates and boxes can make the organization look practical and action oriented but also a little chaotic and unplanned. Other organizations may be located in local government buildings, which can suggest high levels of state funding or a bureaucratic culture.
- **People.** Many persons will hear about your campaign through your staff and volunteers, either formally over the telephone, at receptions or informally in social settings. Thorough briefing and regular updates are required to support effective word-of-mouth communication. No one should be exempt from this. In a snapshot survey of my marketing team at Crisis, only about half of staff and volunteers could immediately remember the charity's core messages.
- **Processes.** A charity wishing to be perceived as efficient and caring can easily be undermined if it has an inefficient and unresponsive customer care system. This means basic things like making sure thank you letters are sent out, that the switchboard operator can easily find the right person and that phones can be answered, or messages left, after hours.
- **Philosophy.** Bruce argues that this is the most important criterion of all and one that is unique to the not-for-profit sector. What we are selling is usually as intangible as an idea or a belief – for example the belief that people should not be forced to sleep rough on our streets. In the absence of a physical product or service, the communication of an organization's vision and values is a core aspect of the campaign.

A campaign will be effectively integrated if it succeeds in making all of these factors work together and reinforce the central, clear and compelling message.

4. **Communications mix.** Not-for-profit organizations can sometimes underestimate the scale and range of their marketing

activities. Although few organizations have the budget to compete with commercial organizations, it is surprising how many communications tools are used by even the smallest charities. At Crisis, for example, a quick checklist would include the following:

- **advertising**: ranging from direct response fundraising to recruitment adverts;
- **personal selling**: through face-to-face fundraising and telemarketing, as well as conferences and events;
- **direct marketing**: whether it is through the mail, newspapers or other media;
- **public relations**: including media relations, the annual report, donor magazines and other literature;
- **exhibitions**: attendance at party conferences or more community-based activity;
- **sponsorship**: including sponsorship of events, publications or services;
- **corporate identity**: expressed, for example, in the logo, strap line and letterheads;
- **sales promotions**: perhaps through cause-related marketing initiatives;
- **new media**: from the use of Web sites to online promotions and e-mail trees;
- **word of mouth**: how you develop ambassadors for your cause among staff, donors or volunteers.

These are some of the tools that will form part of any integrated campaign and, once again, they need to work in the same direction and give out the same message. Careful planning will be required to cope with different lead times as well as multiple objectives and stakeholders.

5. **Creative design.** Effective design will reinforce brand values, key messages and campaign concept. However, creative design is not always the same as effective design. Sometimes creativity can yield first-rate materials which are ineffective or even counter-productive as part of an integrated campaign. This usually occurs where designers are given unclear briefs or where campaign teams have failed to specify the campaign concept clearly enough.

It is important to maintain a critical eye. I was a judge for the *PR Week* Awards and saw more than one example of stunning design which has itself become the object of attention rather than a guide to the organization's key messages.

6. **Internal/external consistency.** As we recognized at the start of the chapter, integrated campaigns can have a beneficial impact within the organization as well as outside it. But this is only the case if messages disseminated internally are consistent with messages conveyed to target publics. Three simple rules should apply. Firstly, campaign objectives and messages must originate from the heart of the organization, rather than exist purely for marketing purposes, otherwise the result will be cynicism and alienation. Secondly, campaign themes should be issues on which there is the prospect of consensus, or the result may be division rather than motivation. Lastly, the organization's behaviour with staff, volunteers and clients must be consistent with its public messages, or it may be accused of double standards.

7. **Financial.** The final item on the checklist is also one of the most important. Integration should be reinforced through budgetary control, which will allow the most effective deployment of resources as well as the delivery of economies of scale. Campaigns devised outside of the budgetary process will need to be managed without this important reinforcement mechanism and may not produce the same results.

WHY IS INTEGRATION SO HARD TO ACHIEVE?

The checklist outlined above has thrown some light on why integration so often fails. Overall, there are five main barriers to effective integration:

▧ **Lack of management support.** Integration relies on the cooperation of managers in a number of different departments. If a campaign does not have the support of senior management, it may struggle to get off the ground or, equally unfortunately, it may be restricted to one department. A key role for the marketing director or chief executive is to influence other stakeholders towards engagement in integrated planning.

▧ **Absence of planning systems.** Sometimes the will exists to run an integrated campaign but the planning systems make collaboration difficult. This can be the case where departmental planning is more robust than corporate planning and where few opportunities exist to influence the plans of other departments. One (temporary) solution to this is to set up a working group spanning the necessary departments.

■ **Lack of ownership.** A campaign is likely to fail if it is not 'owned' by staff across the organization as a whole. This can be the result of power struggles between different departments, especially in organizations in which external relations functions have been split across divisions or departments. In the absence of an appropriate structure, it may be difficult to achieve truly integrated campaigns. (Issues of organizational structure are addressed in Part 1, Chapter 2.)

■ **Poor communication.** Even the most carefully planned campaigns rely on effective internal communication. If staff or volunteers feel poorly informed or too distant from the goals and purpose of the campaign, they will be unable to execute it in their own work, thus eliminating an important aspect of integration. A coherent and effective approach to internal communications is a prerequisite of integrated campaigning.

■ **Product rather than customer focus.** Sometimes a campaign can be undermined by a historical focus on product rather than customers. New ideas are lost as departments continue to work in traditional ways, producing products with which they are familiar rather than those which suit the needs of customers. This can be addressed through the proactive development of a culture of customer orientation and an effective marketing information system.

Having reviewed the process of integration, the rest of the chapter will outline some simple steps to manage integration in practice.

MANAGING INTEGRATION IN PRACTICE

The following is a ten-step guide to managing integration.

Step 1 – planning

Integration is a function of planning rather than a technique for spreading good ideas. It needs to be built into campaigns from the outset, and reinforced through management controls, rather than diffused across the organization once a strategy has been produced. Accordingly, the campaign strategy needs to fit comfortably with an organization's corporate planning processes (see Figure 12.1). It is likely that those corporate strategies will define the parameters of most campaigns. The key question, therefore, is why do you want to run a campaign.

The reasons will vary for different organizations. Crisis has identified the need for a seasonal summer campaign at a time of year when the warm weather relegates homelessness down the list of our target public's priorities. Each year, we devise a campaign concept that is designed primarily to communicate both the relevance and urgency of Crisis' work when it appears least relevant or urgent. This sets the broad parameters for each of our campaigns.

A more overtly campaigning organization like Friends of the Earth may have the objective of achieving legislative change. However, even these kinds of organization have begun to rationalize their public campaigning activity in order to achieve a greater impact on perceptions of the brand. In other words, campaigns serve multiple objectives that need to be balanced according to the requirements of an organization's corporate strategies.

FRIENDS OF THE EARTH

Friends of the Earth established a new planning system in 1997. This has helped them to focus energies and resources to achieve their goals:

■ The strategic plan is big picture and long term, outlining the core corporate goals.
■ Programme strategies take the medium term and highlight how those corporate goals will be achieved.
■ Departmental strategies also take the medium term and illustrate how each function will contribute towards the corporate goals. Operational plans are short term and linked to the annual budget. Integrated marketing campaigns would normally feature at this level.

VISION/PURPOSE

↓

MISSION/VALUES

↓

CORPORATE STRATEGY

↓

MARKETING STRATEGY

↓

CAMPAIGN STRATEGY

Figure 12.1

Once it is clear how campaigns fit with existing corporate plans, then it is essential for clear goals and objectives to be set which are specific, measurable, actionable, realistic and time limited. This will require clarity about the target audience and means of measurement. The more specific the better, so two objectives might be a three percentage point increase in awareness and the generation of £100,000 in voluntary donations from people classified as social groups A and B and living in London.

Everyone involved in planning and executing the campaign must be familiar with these clear goals and understand how their own work will contribute towards achieving them. This understanding will help staff and volunteers interpret the campaign in their own individual work plans.

Step 2 – defining core messages

The next stage is to define key messages for the campaign. This usually works at several different levels:

▇ **One core message.** It is important for campaigns to have a single core message or theme. This should be capable of being summarized in fewer than ten words. For example, our core message is 'lasting solutions to street homelessness'. This is designed to tackle the impression that Crisis only runs emergency services and is reproduced in all communications.

▓ **Three arguments in favour.** The core theme needs to be supported by three main arguments that help to justify the idea being expressed. For example, the Crisis core message is supported by three arguments: 'prevention is better than cure', 'tackle the causes as well as the symptoms of homelessness' and 'help people regain control of their lives'. These arguments develop the theme and help our publics to understand the wide range of services that the charity provides.

▓ **One or more calls to action.** It is not enough to leave target publics with a single message, however powerful it may be. All messages should be supported by a call to action, giving people an idea of what they can do to help. That might range from making a donation to becoming a volunteer or writing to an MP and should be carefully targeted to each audience.

▓ **Anticipate hostile positions.** It is unlikely that campaigns will result wholly in positive messages about any organization. It is much more likely that they will spark questioning and possibly negative or hostile arguments. In all cases, it is important to anticipate those hostile questions. For example, one likely response to a Crisis campaign is to question why we run a shelter for eight days over Christmas when we want to deliver lasting solutions to homelessness.

▓ **Three counter-arguments.** Counter-arguments will need to be prepared for all potential hostile questions in order to effect rapid rebuttal. In the example given above, Crisis would respond that the Christmas shelter stops vulnerable people feeling suicidal at a time of year when their separation from friends or family is most painful. We would also illustrate how the shelter provides solutions, for example, by diagnosing medical conditions such as TB or linking homeless people into resettlement services.

Step 3 – setting up the project team

It is possible that campaigns can be overseen within existing management structures. However, my experience is that it is usually necessary to establish a campaign team with a clear project leader. The project leader would have delegated authority to manage the campaign, usually reporting to the marketing or fundraising director. The composition of that project team will need to include all of the key stakeholders, including representatives from other departments.

The role of the project team is to:

■ construct a project plan and schedule, based on the agreed campaign goals and objectives;
■ appraise the project plan and obtain approval for the allocation of resources;
■ secure ownership for the campaign throughout the organization, by involving other departments in the development of campaign activities;
■ lead internal communications;
■ oversee the management of individual projects that form part of the overall campaign;
■ solve problems;
■ advise on variations from the agreed project plan, due to unforeseen external opportunities or challenges;
■ produce an evaluation of the whole campaign.

The role of the project leader is to:

■ report progress to senior managers;
■ maintain budgetary control;
■ maintain an overview of the project and its intended outcomes;
■ anticipate problems and suggest corrective actions;
■ ensure that deadlines are kept;
■ support members of the project team.

The composition of the project team will vary depending on the size of the organization and the importance of the campaign. A smaller charity may be reliant on the proactive involvement of trustees and other volunteers. In fact, it can be useful to broaden the team by inviting external contacts to be ad hoc members or even form an advisory group. This might be advisable in order to boost specialist expertise (eg on a specific issue), provide an expert sounding board or broaden ownership (perhaps by involving a trustee). It is usually possible to find experienced people prepared to give up a limited amount of time to attend occasional meetings and to be available at the end of a telephone or e-mail.

CULTURAL TRENDS

Cultural Trends is a journal produced by the Policy Studies Institute, a think-tank.

Marketing management of the journal is delegated to the director of publishing, who has formed a small project team involving the editor and specialists in research, finance and communications.

Although the editor is responsible for the content of the journal, the project manager is responsible for the marketing campaigns built around it, including conferences, events, public relations, media relations, direct marketing and advertising.

The project manager has also developed an editorial board, which consists of experts in some of the fields of interest to *Cultural Trends*, including the film industry, the built heritage and the music business. The board members meet regularly to advise on campaigns but are not paid by the institute.

Step 4 – developing the project plan

The team's first task is to devise a project plan and schedule. This usually forms three stages:

▨ **Generating creative ideas.** It is important that staff are given the opportunity to contribute ideas to the campaign whilst it is still in the planning stages. One of the responsibilities of individual project team members may be to organize brainstorming sessions at departmental team meetings, which allows good ideas to be sourced from different parts of the organization. This is much more likely to generate ownership of the campaign as a whole. The project team can then focus on assessing the ideas that have been put forward and generating ideas to fill any perceived gaps.

▨ **Mapping out the campaign.** A detailed project plan will need to be constructed in order to oversee the campaign. Ideally this should take the form of a GANTT chart or similar, indicating the interdependency of different elements of each activity. One of the critical functions of the project team will be to manage these interdependencies, for example by ensuring that data lists and campaign literature have been produced in good time for mailings. This GANTT chart will therefore be a central part of project team meetings.

▓ **Commissioning work.** The project team will commission work from its members and from other parts of the organization. For example, research may need to be produced, logos developed, campaign literature drafted, etc. Perhaps the easiest way to proceed is to adopt an account management system, by which an individual member of the project team assumes responsibility for commissioning and overseeing the work of one or more colleagues, wherever they are located in the organization. This simplifies project management and enables the account handler to provide updates on key activities at the request of the project manager.

Step 5 – allocating resources

It is likely that a dedicated sum will have been set aside for the campaign and this will need to be allocated by the project team. Responsibility for this should rest with the project leader once the team has made a cost-benefit appraisal of the initiatives being proposed by the different departments. The project team may request more detailed information from those departments before assigning resources. This commissioning relationship should strengthen both the ownership of the campaign and the delivery of individual activities.

The campaign is likely to have a wider impact within the organization. For example, the personnel manager may wish to use the campaign in training or team-building activity. The project team should take a proactive approach towards identifying opportunities for extending the campaign throughout the organization, as departments may not have realized the opportunities presented by their existing work plans. Ideally, the objectives of the campaign will inform the operational planning process, allowing managers throughout the organization to interpret the campaign in their own areas of activity, coordinated by the project team. This would require a lead time of around six to nine months.

One way to generate added value for the campaign is to negotiate strategic alliances with external contacts. For example, the music satellite channel MTV has made an advertisement for one of Crisis' campaigns and broadcast it on the channel. This would have been beyond the reach of the campaign budget.

Step 6 – obtaining stakeholders

Before going public with a campaign, it is important to brief stake-holders, answer any questions they may have about your initiative and commission them to act as ambassadors.

Word-of-mouth communication is a key ingredient of any campaign but in order for it to work on your behalf, staff or volunteers need to understand the purpose of the campaign, be familiar with key messages and be ready to answer any awkward questions. However, it is also important that people are forewarned about major initiatives. If staff do not know that there is going to be a media launch on a certain day, they would not reinforce your main messages. If they have not seen newspaper adverts or donor mail shots in advance, they would not have had time to understand what you are trying to do in their own words. This can be a tremendous missed opportunity. Although Crisis has only about 50 staff, it has a network of nearly 5,000 volunteers. But it is in the 1990s that it has begun to communicate with volunteers on a strategic level.

- ▓ **Staff.** It is useful to organize a briefing for staff at least a couple of months in advance of a major campaign. In my experience, staff find the theory useful but are most interested in seeing what the campaign looks like, in terms of visuals and products. One of the best ways to brief staff about a campaign can therefore be to distribute campaign materials and discuss people's reactions. Team meetings can be a good vehicle for this. A question-and-answer sheet is also vital.
- ▓ **Volunteers.** It is important to have a robust communications system with volunteers. Crisis has introduced a biannual newspaper that details major campaigns. However, it follows this up with tailored briefing letters as appropriate and key volunteers like school speakers are briefed face to face and given the same campaign pack as staff.
- ▓ **Donors.** Warm donors may expect to hear about campaigns directly from the organization they support, rather than second hand through the media or from a friend. It may be worth considering forewarning donors in a newsletter or magazine or using a pre-campaign appeal to build support. The launch of a campaign will usually result in large numbers of telephone calls, which should be answered immediately.

Step 7 – creating an impact

Creating an initial impact usually involves organizing a launch and this is something the not-for-profit sector often does with great imagination. There are seven standard ingredients that usually combine to good effect in getting a campaign off the drawing board:

■ **Research.** It is often helpful to have some up-to-date research that illustrates the key points you are trying to make. Ten years ago, the sector sometimes got away with publishing flimsy research. Today, media scrutiny ensures that all research must be robust and academically sound. It is far better not to publish at all, if research does not stand up to analysis. However, many parts of the media, especially broadsheets and the trade press, will expect an original angle, which is most likely to come from quantitative research.

■ **Case studies.** As the not-for-profit sector mainly deals in issues and ideas, it is likely that campaigns will focus on the needs or experiences of people. At a launch, it is vital if possible to have access to real people who can tell their own story. This is essential for broadcast coverage and will be the most powerful statement of your case. It is worth investing time in researching and preparing case studies and briefing people about what to expect when they talk to journalists. (See Chapter 8 on PR for more about this.)

■ **Celebrity.** A well-chosen celebrity can help grab attention for your launch, especially if you can find one who has some connection with the issue you are presenting. Some organizations have developed long-standing associations with celebrities who are involved in their field of work. Emma Thompson's role of patron of Alone in London and Caroline Aherne's support for the Retinoblastoma Society have helped to raise the profile of both organizations.

■ **Endorsement.** It can also help if a campaign is given endorsement, although care needs to be taken about where that support is coming from. The launch of a new service can often benefit from the endorsement of the relevant Minister of State. This is especially true in today's era of government in which some charity work is being openly questioned (eg the government's street tsar sparked controversy in 1999 about the value of soup runs for homeless people). However, a campaign targeted at the City would also benefit from the support of a leading figure from the world of finance.

■ **Venue.** Many people will be persuaded to attend a launch because of the venue rather than the content! The ideal location is one that matches the messages of the campaign but is somewhere that members of the target audience may never have visited. Good examples might include underground London, one of the Livery Halls or the top of the BT tower. (Venue finding is discussed in Chapter 9.)

■ **Audience.** The last ingredient is also the most important. Who is the launch for? Who do you wish to attend? And what will you ask them to do after you have presented your campaign?

■ **Timing.** Timing is critical, not only time of day and the time of the week but also the timing of your other marketing activity. This will be worked through in the project plan and will vary according to your campaign. However, it is likely that you will want to orchestrate your other marketing initiatives to coincide with the publicity generated by your launch, so that your target audience is given the opportunity to act.

JEANS FOR GENES CAMPAIGN

Great Ormond Street and three smaller charities got together to promote a campaign for genetic research.

In 1998, they persuaded Robbie Williams to be photographed wearing jeans that had been painted onto his body.

The photographs were used throughout the national and regional media, creating huge impact from very little cost.

Robbie also featured prominently in accompanying materials for that year's campaign.

Step 8 – sustaining impact

Although not-for-profit organizations are usually very good at staging imaginative launches, they are often much poorer at sustaining the momentum of campaigns. This should be a major element of the project plan.

It is essential for organizations to keep a couple of aces up their sleeves and resist the temptation to use all their best campaign materials to support the launch. Instead, campaigns should be viewed as a programme of activities over a sustained period of weeks or months.

After creating that initial impact, it is important to schedule other campaign materials very carefully. Research publications, events, mail shots, advertising and conferences should be timetabled carefully so that interest in the campaign can be prolonged.

A useful approach has been adopted by the Royal National Institute for the Blind (RNIB) that has recognized that it is not possible for organizations with limited resources to sustain a high profile throughout the year. The RNIB have introduced regular 'heightened awareness periods' – or HAPs – which they use to focus resources behind campaign messages. Research has demonstrated that the RNIB successfully raises its profile during these HAPs. Moreover, the regular timing of HAPs throughout the year helps the charity to maintain its increased recognition levels.

Step 9 – campaign management

One function of the project team is to decide how to handle the unexpected. This task is made much easier if information is provided at regular intervals.

During 1995, Barnardo's, the childcare charity, ran a campaign around the 150th birthday of Thomas Barnardo. The aim of the campaign was to explain why the charity had stopped running children's homes and illustrate some of its modern-day work.

In preparing for the campaign, the project team had identified a number of measures which could be tracked on a regular basis and which would indicate whether the campaign was working. These measures were studied regularly and helped the team to take decisions about the forward schedule.

For example, the transmission of three programmes about Barnardo's on BBC 1 could have had a negative impact on perceptions of the charity by drawing more attention to the past. In fact, press measurement during the transmissions revealed that over 70 per cent of stories had focused on the charity's modern work. The project team had a number of initiatives ready to run which would help focus attention on modern aspects of the charity's work. Because the press measurement was favourable, these initiatives were scheduled later in the campaign, helping to sustain interest and move our messages forward. (Evaluation is tackled in more detail in Chapter 11.)

However, the project team was also able to consider how the campaign could be adjusted to take advantage of unexpected opportunities. Initially, the Barnardo's project team had decided that a reunion of 600 ex-Barnardo's 'boys and girls' was too risky to be used proactively in the campaign, as it would focus too much attention on the past. However, the positive reception given to the three BBC programmes allowed the event to be used constructively in media work.

Step 10 – evaluation

The last section has highlighted the importance of ongoing measurement, which is the subject of a separate chapter of this book. However, it is worth emphasizing once again the need to appraise key measures throughout the campaign, rather than after it has finished. This might take several forms: donor feedback, media content measurement, monthly awareness measurement, 'favourability' ratings, etc. Many of these forms of measurement are now quite affordable, as groups of charities have clubbed together to form benchmark groups. Even the best-laid plans will need to be adjusted following feedback. Measurement should therefore be regarded as a tool of campaign management rather than a necessary postscript.

REFERENCES

Bruce (1998) *Successful Charity Marketing*, ICSA/Prentice-Hall
Kotler *et al* (1999) *Principles of Marketing*, Prentice-Hall
Smith, Bery and Pulford (1999) *Strategic Marketing Communications*, Kogan Page
Wall (2000) Does your charity take dirty money? *Big Issue*, 24–30 January

13

Advertising

Paula Keaveney

Advertising, like PR, is a promotional tool that can be used as part of the marketing mix. It has many benefits. Unlike media coverage in which a journalist has interpreted what a charity says, the message in an advertisement is 100 per cent controllable. The crude difference is one of cost. When an advertisement is placed in print or broadcast media, the cinema or elsewhere, the advertiser, in this case the charity, has paid for the opportunity. Charities wanting to advertise need to think very carefully about the costs and benefits. Involvement in advertising is neither cheap nor quick, and while a team of in-house experts is not always necessary, there will be a steep learning curve for newcomers to this activity.

Firstly, it is important to be accurate about terminology. Many people use the term 'advertise' when what they in fact mean is 'promote'. Advertising is a paid-for message, which appears in the media, owned by someone else. An article about a charity in its own magazine is not advertising. Neither is it advertising when a press release written by the charity is used by a journalist in the local newspaper. This remains the case even if the release is printed in its entirety without editing.

Precision about the definition of advertising is not merely semantics. Mistakes in this area can lead to hefty bills and confusion about areas of responsibility. It is also vital that charity trustees, and others who may desire more publicity, are aware that the nature of advertising involves cost. Given that charities involved in advertising are likely to deal with a number of outside agencies, it is also important that the definitions are completely understood at the outset.

WHY ADVERTISE? – BENEFITS AND PITFALLS

The main benefits of advertising are:

- Control – the advertiser decides the message and delivery, and chooses the media.
- Audience – the choice of media can be made to reach a specific audience.
- Reach – some media will never carry editorial about the charity but will happily take an advertisement.
- Impact – adverts can appear in many more places than the traditional news media. Bus shelters, roadside poster sites, tube trains, travel tickets… the list is ever growing.

However, the major problem of any advertising campaign is the need to ensure enough repetition. With the exception of those that are really news stories in disguise, advertisements should never appear only once. To absorb any message properly, we need to hear it, or see it, a number of times. The parallel of exam revision is useful here. Anyone who has learned a subject, and revised it for a test, knows that it takes a number of reviews before enough has been 'taken in'. Advertisers want their viewers, or readers, to take in a message well enough to prompt action. This is why repetition is vital.

Unfortunately, it is not just repetition that matters. Advertisers need to make sure that the message is being repeated frequently enough, within the right time period and to the right audience. Media-buying experts will be able to make recommendations based on the number of 'opportunities to see' provided by particular segments of the media.

Clearly, advertising needs both repetition and enough external advice on placement if it is to be effective. It is also painfully obvious that the cost of an effective advertising campaign will be greatly affected by the need for repetition. Equally obvious is that the many one-off opportunities that present themselves will not deliver an effective campaign.

If a charity is unable to afford the necessary repetition, or perhaps it should be called reinforcement, it would be well advised to think twice about whether it is worth advertising at all.

Many charities do advertise, however, and even without prospects of a campaign, it is worth being aware of the tools, techniques and issues involved when a marketing campaign does require paid-for advertising. The rest of this chapter looks at some of the techniques and issues and touches on ways in which charities without an advertising budget can nevertheless make some gains in this area.

ADVERTISING – WHAT IS ON OFFER?

Advertising in the print media

With the exception of recruitment advertisements (see below) most charity advertisements are placed to raise funds. These can elicit a straightforward donation or a request for something like a legacy pack. The Disasters Emergency Committee (DEC) advertisements are a good example of a donation request. The DEC is a group of overseas aid charities that take joint action to raise funds at times of high-profile overseas disasters. The DEC ads tend to contain a simple message about the crisis and a return form so that people can donate money as a result of reading the advertisement. Codes on each ad allow staff to monitor which treatments or media yield the best response.

Print media advertising can be costly and can yield surprisingly poor results. Unless a series of ads is booked, there is little chance to get the repetition needed. And yet charity advertisements in the national press remain very common. This is because those buying the space are often able to get last-minute slots at what are called 'distress rates'. These are slots that the media owner has not been able to sell and are thus going cheap.

Advertising in the broadcast media

An increasing number of charities are using, or piloting, direct response advertising on radio or TV. The purpose of this advertising is to elicit a response from the listener or viewer. The request is usually for a straightforward donation, but can be offering the chance to register for specific information. In every case, there is a telephone number that is repeated. Charities interested in trying out this form of advertising would be well advised to talk to others who have done so recently. Oxfam and the National Canine Defence League are examples. Charities with experience in this area may be able to suggest agencies to approach, or to avoid. Before any advertisement is produced, a charity will need to work out exactly how telephone calls will be dealt with. There are external organizations which can do with this, and it is vital that calls can be answered quickly and professionally. Because of this element, the responsibility for direct response TV or radio is often given to the staff member responsible for direct mail and telemarketing.

Broadcast advertisements by charities in the United Kingdom are subject to restrictions by the Independent Television Commission and the Radio Authority. The details of these are contained in publications that are available free of charge from the two organizations.

The restrictions cover a range of issues including content, tone and style. The ITC code makes it clear that advertisements for charities must:

▩ handle with care and discretion matters likely to arouse strong emotions in the audience;
▩ not suggest that anyone will lack proper feeling or fail in any responsibility through not supporting a charity;
▩ respect the dignity of those on whose behalf an appeal is being made;
▩ not address any fundraising message specifically to children;
▩ not contain comparisons with other charities;
▩ avoid presenting an exaggerated impression of the scale or nature of the social problem to which the work of the charity is addressed, for example by illustrating the message with non-typical extreme cases;
▩ not mislead in any way as to the field of activity of the charity or the use to which donations will be put.

In some cases, it may be a commercial company that is the advertiser. A company may, for example, be offering to donate a proportion of product sales to charity. In this case, it is the company that 'owns' the advertisement, but there are still rules in the ITC code:

■ There must be evidence that the charity concerned has agreed to the advertising.
■ It must be clear which charities are benefiting and there must be a clear way in which any proportion of proceeds to be donated is worked out.
■ There cannot be offers like this linked with medicinal products.

(In early 2001, the UK Government drafted broadcasting legislation that may have an impact on some of the regulatory bodies and their restrictions. While there will be no immediate changes, charities embarking on advertising after 2001 would be advised to check the situation.)

Adverts in disguise

Many magazines and newspapers carry pages headed 'advertising feature'. These are written in the style of the publication's editorial pages and sometimes carry supportive advertising. As 'advertising features', this space has been paid for. Charities contacted about taking part in an 'advertorial' should be aware of this and ensure staff enquire about any cost involved before sending any editorial material. Advertorials are often used proactively by national charities during special weeks, when there is a need to appear in as many regional papers as possible.

There is also some crossover in the world of broadcasting. For example, syndicated programmes produced for local and regional commercial radio can involve payment for inclusion. In these cases, it is again important for staff to ensure they are aware of any payments involved before any work is done with the programme.

Listings

There is a wide range of publications, including sites on the Internet, which offer charities the chance to take a listing, or a display advertisement. These publications are often highly targeted directories (for example a book being sent to all directors of social service departments). Many charities order repeat entries without thinking. It is vital that these listings are considered as part of an overall strategy. Charities should ensure they adequately monitor the source of contacts, so that the effectiveness of listings publications can be measured. There may be more effective ways of using that money. It is worth also trying to find out from a reader, or from any survey material, exactly how its audience uses the publication. Research has, for example, thrown some doubt on the usefulness for legacy fundraisers of inclusion in lawyers' directories.

Outdoor advertising and ambient media

Outdoor advertising includes poster sites and bus shelters. Ambient media tend to mean anything that can carry advertising and are not already categorized. The back of a bus ticket is an example of ambient media. There are some very creative opportunities open to charities using this type of advertising, but it is an area in which expert advice and figures on opportunities to see are vital.

Free advertisements – as PR tools

Despite the nature of advertising involving payment, there are occasions on which charities can advertise free.

Ad agencies will sometimes offer to produce a one-off, and to get space donated for an advertisement to run once. These opportunities are nearly always the product of a larger campaign and the advertisements themselves are really produced as news stories.

An excellent example of this was Save the Children's 75th birthday TV ad. As an advertisement, the item was shown just once. It featured HRH the Princess Royal talking directly to camera. The royal participation created a news story. The advertisement may have only made one commercial appearance, but it appeared repeatedly in news programmes, was written about in the national press and was a good radio talking point. There is more about the advertising PR link in Chapter 8 on public relations. It is worth bearing in mind that advertisements designed to prompt news stories do not have to be free. A charity may decide to spend on either a single or series of controversial advertisements with PR in mind.

Free advertisements – as opportunities

Charities without the budget to place advertisements but with the capacity to design and reproduce a simple ad, can take advantage of the times when publications cannot sell all their space. A targeted letter, plus advertisement for use, to a range of publications can result in inclusion. This tactic has been used by NCH and by the Muscular Dystrophy Campaign. Charities taking this approach need to bear in mind that it is speculative and that the date of use cannot be predetermined. This means advertisements that will not date quickly are preferred.

Recruitment advertising – the hidden opportunity

Even big charities with large marketing departments will have relatively small advertising budgets. Most will not be able to sustain the level of repeat mentions and audience reach needed for a major, effective campaign, yet these charities have advertisements in the national and regional press several times every week.

More people will get their idea of a charity through seeing recruitment advertisements than from any other source. Recruitment advertisements are a major part of the public presence of a charity. They carry the logo and should carry a consistent and compelling message. Yet, in most cases, such ads are not seen as part of the marketing mix and are very much the property of staff with little marketing knowledge.

If a charity wants to improve its advertising effectiveness at no extra cost, the simplest way would be to ensure that recruitment advertising is seen as an important part of the marketing effort and given the internal value that involves.

ADVERTISING – HOW TO GET STARTED AND HOW TO FIND OUT MORE

There are no right or wrong answers about advertising. There are, however, steps charities can take to make sure they avoid the obvious pitfalls and make the most of any opportunities:

▨ Find another charity that uses advertising in the way your charity needs, or thinks it needs, and ask for feedback on how it has worked for them.

▧ Read articles about charity advertising. *Professional Fundraising Magazine* often has items but it is worth also looking at back copies of trade papers like *Campaign* and *Media Week*.

▧ Get information from the ITC, the Radio Authority and the Advertising Standards Authority.

▧ Think about agencies. At the very least you will need an agency to place the advertisements. You are also likely to need one to create the ad. Some agencies will offer a full service and do everything. Some may have working arrangements with other firms. It is worth taking advice from other charities about this.

And above everything else, define:

▧ what you want to say to whom;
▧ what you want them to do as a result;
▧ how you will measure success;
▧ how much money you have to spend.

Good luck.

14

Database marketing for voluntary organizations – databases and why they matter

Peter Larsen

In database terms, size is not really an issue. Since the late 1980s, organizations of all sizes have recognized their customer database as a major organizational asset. There has been an increasing reliance on computer systems to run many aspects of the business. The volume of data collected about customers and about the organization's interaction with them makes it virtually impossible for a charity to manage its relationship with supporters efficiently without the aid of a database. A good database enhances the charity's ability to develop relationships with supporters through better service and through the appropriate fundraising strategies. This chapter provides an overview of 'how to manage the process' of selecting and implementing a new database system for small to medium-sized organizations.

GETTING STARTED (SOME THINGS TO WATCH OUT FOR)

A hazard of database projects can be the use of technical jargon to communicate system features to non-technical users. Such poor communication practice can lead to costly problems. Potential suppliers who cannot explain the features and benefits of their software may be inappropriate partners. Because your working relationship is likely to span several years, it is important to see your supplier as a partner. In a relatively short time, your database will be an important business tool. And here is the crux. Your specialist knowledge of your organization, its objectives, fundraising plans and working practices makes you and your colleagues best qualified to specify the capabilities of the database.

Database projects need dedicated leadership. Technology skills are not the issue – business knowledge is. Whatever the size of your organization, adopt a top-down approach and give a senior manager responsibility for leading the project. Introducing a database system is so important that the project must be clearly led.

WHAT IS A DATABASE?

Definitions abound. To keep it simple, a database is a collection of records maintained on a computer system, which is structured so that it can be constantly updated or enhanced from other sources. The data collection supports a range of applications allowing any part of the data to be used for any purpose, at any time.

Some may prefer to shroud this issue in mystique, but it is straightforward. It is just technology's way of imitating cognitive human processes and good working practice. Databases provide a virtual team with valuable skill sets such as:

▓ a librarian who structures the data so that it is consistently stored, systematically archived and easy to retrieve and work with;
▓ a clerical officer with a good filing system maintaining an accurate record of communications with the supporters;
▓ a marketing executive grouping the data together so that trends and patterns can be quickly spotted;

▓ a sales executive managing communication with supporters using Rolodex cards and a diary to plan their activity.

WHAT YOU SHOULD EXPECT OF A DATABASE – ITS VALUE TO YOUR ORGANIZATION

There are many ways to exploit your database and many organizations still under-utilize them. At a high level, consider the core marketing functions. If you treat the database as a direct channel to supporters, you can overlay those basic objectives onto your database.

▓ It helps build your brand with your core audience.
▓ It develops good relationships with supporters by allowing you to distribute appropriate, personalized information.
▓ It enhances good supporter service through access to reliable information.
▓ It becomes a major source of income.

Continuing this theme, we shall place database functionality in the context of voluntary organizations and characterize the advantages it offers under some general headings.

Contact management

Managing and maintaining accurate records of your communication with supporters and any responses they make to them (financial and non-financial) begins a process of performance measurement which informs you about:

▓ the efficacy of the different approaches you make;
▓ the willingness of different supporters to react when prompted.

Supporter services

By systematically recording the interests, the likes/dislikes and preferences of each supporter and tracking any changes to those characteristics, you will be better able to manage each relationship effectively and create a personalized communication programme based on supporter choice.

Raising funds

Appeals, legacies, capital appeals, committed giving, sponsored events are just some of the projects that benefit from a database. All can be easily managed and monitored using a decent system. As the database develops, you can apply statistical techniques to segment your supporter base so your fundraising runs on robust 'return on investment' (ROI) criteria.

Event management

Linking event organizers, volunteers, licensing authorities, local groups, the publicity campaign and the attributable income will provide two benefits:

▩ You will get an event-management planning template for future events.
▩ You will quickly identify which events are likely to be most profitable.

Financial transaction processing

The database may not manage the processing of money, although more advanced systems will, but it should maintain up-to-date and reliable records of all income streams. Linked to other bits of data (see the preceding headings), a history of financial payments and non-payments is a vital component for identifying high net worth individuals amongst the supporter base.

Management reporting

All staff need accurate information – budget holders in particular need it to support decision making. Organizations need consistency across the enterprise. Your database should provide timely and easy access to key performance indicators to inform planning, developing new programmes and budget reviews.

WHAT YOU SHOULD NOT EXPECT FROM A DATABASE – AND WHY

The database provides a safe home for your data. It allows you to maintain, update and change the data, and by providing easy access, manipulate it.

Aside from that, it must provide easy import and export data facilities so you can take advantage of the best tools on the market to run all the data-related tasks efficiently.

Your database can provide routines that automate the most common tasks such as generating new supporter records, amending existing ones, verifying addresses, recording payments made by supporters, creating and exporting contact lists for communications, etc. But your database is not designed to be a spreadsheet, a report writer, a statistical analysis package or a word processor. Yes, you can have these functions embedded into your system but they are unlikely to be as well developed as a specialist software package. There are affordable tools that can be quickly integrated with the database so that even the smallest organization can use advanced techniques. The important thing is your database can link to them easily.

THE KEY REQUIREMENTS

Your database needs to be flexible because your demands on the system will change. The technology must be scaleable so that the system can grow with the organization. It needs to be able to run on different types of computer hardware. That means you can take advantage of technological developments. It should be designed for use by non-technical staff and the underlying technology should be well supported. Avoid systems based on obscure programming languages that will leave you at the mercy of a small number of technical specialists when problems arise.

All databases need the following principal features:

▓ support a flexible data structure;
▓ provide robust data import (online and batch routines);
▓ high quality name and address handling;
▓ established campaign and promotion management;

- ■ definable contact management facilities;
- ■ easy to use event tracking;
- ■ basic decision support;
- ■ links to other software in the organization (Finance, Supporter Services, etc);
- ■ routines for links to external agencies (BACS, mailing house, etc);
- ■ scaleable;
- ■ not technology dependent.

It is worth creating your own checklist and using it to drive any preliminary discussion you have with potential suppliers.

INITIAL CONSIDERATIONS WHEN LOOKING FOR A DATABASE

Where will it be located?

Do you want your database running at your offices or at a bureau as a facilities management (FM) service? An in-house solution provides greater control but means initial capital expenditure (CAPEX) and variable costs of maintenance and development. Conversely, FM solutions can minimize CAPEX and fixed running costs. FM solutions that were traditionally more suited to larger organizations are now an option for all through Internet-based application hosting.

How do I get what I want?

There are two basic alternatives, with a 'third way' worth considering:

1. **Shrink-wrapped software.** There are lots of packages designed for not-for-profit organizations and they provide functionality designed to meet the recurring demands of potential users. They are homogeneous. They are unlikely to match your requirements exactly but, unless your working practice is significantly different from others in the sector, they provide most of the basic requirements at a relatively low entry cost.

2. **A bespoke solution.** Use your knowledge and experience to define exactly what the database has to deliver. Well managed, it is an approach that will provide a database that does exactly what you want. Contemporary development techniques and more affordable technology make it a realistic option, but be aware that some of your effort could well be wasted as some part of your 'design' will inevitably replicate existing software functionality.

3. **'A third way'.** The first two alternatives have merits and weaknesses. It is worth considering a hybrid approach that effectively uses the best components of a package format and integrates them with software designed to your own specification. This 'best of breed' approach is common in other sectors. It requires adaptive thinking and an experienced project management resource. It necessitates knowledge of the total database marketing (rather than the not-for-profit) software market and some fairly advanced technical skills. If you have access to such knowledge, you can get the best possible return from a bespoke system that fully meets your requirements and makes efficient use of your budget.

SOME STEPS TO HELP SELECT YOUR DATABASE

▓ Take system users' opinions. Start by taking the opinions of all current and potential users of the database through individual interviews. Use a structured questionnaire to find out:
  - what they do with the current system (if any) and what they need of a new one;
  - when they do it – how long it takes them and how often they have to do it;
  - how it works in practice and if they feel there are better ways of doing it.

  Trust their input on basic design features, screen layout, system navigation and so on. Have them outline their ideal system and an acceptable one. Experienced system users seem to understand ergonomics better than the specialist designers do.

▓ Create a statement of requirements (SOR). This important document becomes the project 'oracle'. As well as some background about the organization and the need for a database, it must describe in very specific terms what the system has to deliver, the data it needs to maintain, who the database users are, what it will be used for, how it will be used, and any links to other computer systems, internal and remote. Be prepared for this to take time. It is a vital part of the process. An unambiguous SOR is a worthwhile investment. It is the basis for inviting potential suppliers to tender for your business. At a basic level, there are only three parts to database implementation – define, create, implement. The SOR is the major task at the definition stage. It is worth considering that around 40 per cent of the budget for all database projects is eaten up by the software (create stage). It is best to deal with anomalies before then.

■ Test load. Once you have a short list of potential suppliers, require them to give a practical demonstration of their solution at your premises using some of your data. If this cannot be done now, there may be a similar difficulty in implementing the real system.

■ Structured fact-finds. Talk, confidentially, to other organizations that have worked with them – ideally not from the list of clients provided by the supplier. Take anecdotal notes but use prepared questions.

■ Scorecard. Compare alternatives on a like-for-like basis by using a risk management check list (scorecard) to differentiate. Grade the factors from low to high risk, with a weighted scale for each.

■ Expect and plan for change. Databases and the use you will put them to are like much else – protean in nature. While the speed of change will vary across organizations, the need for them will be reasonably constant. That is partly why flexibility is an important system feature. Technological advances occur at such speed that we can all look a bit silly in hindsight, even big organizations.

■ Feel the difference. Learn to differentiate between data, information and knowledge:
  – Data is raw, cumbersome and awkward to deal with, eg a list of names and addresses.
  – Information is created by interrogating the data, eg a report showing how many addresses appear in each region.
  – Knowledge is our attempt to understand the information, eg which region produces the highest level of income per household.

■ Some hints – current techniques make screens easy to design. Do not buy a database exclusively on how it looks. Although it is important that users feel comfortable with their database, it is vital not to get sidetracked by smoke and mirrors.

Initial costs of shrink-wrapped packages look more affordable but there will be inevitable 'extras', for modifications, loading your data, set up and installation. Do obtain a full breakdown of all ancillary costs.

■ Consider topping up your skills by working with a consultant at key stages.

SOME TRENDS TO BE AWARE OF

More affordable and powerful technology has been a major cause of the huge increase in the volume of data stored around the world. The big picture is worth considering. In the early 1990s, it was estimated that the volume stored globally doubled every 20 months. Estimates suggest that this now occurs in less than 12 months. More data does not lead to better information. In fact, it becomes more difficult to create meaning, and organizational knowledge suffers in consequence. All sizes of organization face this dilemma. Those who meet the challenge of providing decision makers with reliable information at the right time succeed.

It is not a technology issue. System performance and machine capacity advance relentlessly. Our role is to use these tools as best we can by adopting sound procedures and good working practices. Whether you intend to run a database on a single PC or a small internal network, the efficacy of your database will be a function of how well you use it.

Expect to make some mistakes along the way. Even the biggest organizations have made them on database projects. There is not a foolproof method for selecting the right database. The system that is best for you is the one that provides the best return. You can measure that by striking a balance between your ideals and what can be delivered within your budget.

AN OPTIMISTIC NOTE FOR SMALLER ORGANIZATIONS

You may be considering setting up your first database. Perhaps you feel that the size of your organization means this chapter does not apply and the examples have no direct bearing on your particular circumstances. You may well be right, but there are points worthy of your further consideration.

The application of data to drive the marketing function has gone through many changes, some of them merely linguistic. 'Database marketing' gave way in the mid-1990s to 'relationship marketing'. That process has now been redefined and described as 'customer relationship marketing'. Techniques evolve and the way the data is used changes, but the underlying principle has an entirely yester-year feel. Big organizations have simply adopted the business model operated by well-run corner shops:

■ They have put the customer (supporter) at the centre of their operation.
■ They get to know their customers and their personal circumstances.
■ They enhance their relationship with them through good service.
■ They watch what they buy and try to anticipate what they will want next time.
■ They check what they spend and make offers to get them to spend a little more.
■ They thank them for their business and they mean it.
■ They know when to back off and leave well alone.

Big enterprises invest large sums of money attempting to deal with their many customers as individuals. The numbers may not be as high for the small organization but the principle and the practice are identical and a good database plays a key role in the process. (Membership schemes and relationship marketing are discussed in more detail in Chapter 6.)

Appendix 1

Further reading

ON MARKETING AND CHARITY MARKETING IN GENERAL

Bruce, I (1998) *Successful Charity Marketing*, ICSA/Prentice-Hall
Kotler *et al* (1999) *Principles of Marketing*, Prentice-Hall

The *Marketing in Action* series, published by Kogan Page, includes a number of specialist books of relevance to marketing practitioners.

The *International Journal of Nonprofit and Voluntary Sector Marketing* (Henry Stewart Publications) carries articles on a wide range of marketing issues, including research on trends.

ON THE STATUTORY SECTOR

Forrester and Pilch (1998) *A Guide to Funding from Government Departments and Agencies*, Directory of Social Change
Sluiter and Wattier (1999) *A Guide to European Union Funding*, Directory of Social Change

ON FUNDRAISING IN GENERAL

Mullin (1997) *Fundraising Strategy*, ICFM
Passingham (1997) *Tried and Tested Ideas for Raising Money Locally*,
  Directory of Social Change
A Guide to the Major Trusts, (three volumes) Directory of Social
  Change

Trusts Monitor, published by the Directory of Social Change, is a
magazine produced three times a year concentrating on charitable
trusts and foundations.

Smith, G (1997) *Asking Properly*, White Lion Press

Professional Fundraising magazine, T and D Press, covers news and
information about fundraising in the not-for-profit sector.

The Institute of Charity Fundraising Managers publishes a
monthly newsletter covering news as well as updates on relevant
legislation and the organization's activities.

The UK Fundraising Web site (www.fundraising.org.uk) carries
regularly changing news of use to fundraisers.

ON WORKING WITH POLITICIANS

Child, S *Politico's Guide to Parliament*
Curry, D *Lobbying Government*, Chartered Institute of Housing
De Souza, C *So You Want to be a Lobbyist*
Lattimer (2000) *The Campaigning Handbook 2000*, Directory of Social
  Change
Miller, C *Political Lobbying*
Morris, P *Legitimate Lobbying*
White, J (ed) *Politics on the Internet*
Wilson, D *The A-Z of Campaigning*

The House of Commons Information Office and House of Lords
Information Office both publish useful fact sheets on parliamentary procedure. Both offices can be contacted on 020 7219 3000.

Vacher's *Parliamentary Companion*
Vacher's *European Companion*
PMS *Parliamentary Companion*
Dod's Parliamentary Companion
Roth, A *Parliamentary Profiles*
Times Guide to the House of Commons (1997 edn)
Walter, R *The Almanac of British Politics*

ON NEW MEDIA AND THE INTERNET

Lake (2000) *Fundraising on the Internet*
Watson (1998) *Making Sense of the Internet*, National Institute for
Social Work

ON MEMBERSHIP SCHEMES, RELATIONSHIPS AND DIRECT MAIL

Burnett, K (1992) *Relationship Fundraising*, White Lion Press
Burnett, K (1997) *Friends for Life*, White Lion Press
Peppers, D and Rogers, M (1993) *The One-to-One Future*, Piatkus
Books

ON PUBLIC RELATIONS AND MARKETING COMMUNICATIONS IN GENERAL

Ali (1999) *The DIY Guide to Public Relations*, Directory of Social
Change
Smith, B and Pulford (1999) *Strategic Marketing Communications*,
Kogan Page

PR Week magazine and the IPR's magazine *Profile* both publish
case studies of effective PR campaigns run by not-for-profit organizations.

ON CORPORATE FUNDRAISING

Morton (1999) *Corporate Fundraising*, ICFM/CAF

Corporate Citizen magazine, published by the Directory of Social Change, is a useful way of keeping in touch with company–charity link-ups.

Smyth (2000) *The Guide to UK Company Giving*, Directory of Social Change

ON CHARITY LAW

Bates, Wells and Braithwaite and the Centre for Voluntary Sector Development (2000) *The Fundraiser's Guide to the Law*, published in association with the Charities Aid Foundation
Claricoat and Philips (1998) *Charity Law A to Z*, Jordans
Ticher (2000) *Data Protection for Voluntary Organizations*, Directory of Social Change

ON CHARITIES, CHARITY ORGANIZATION AND CHARITY MANAGEMENT

Third Sector magazine and *Charity Times* magazine both cover news and issues across the whole range of charity management. Third Sector also publishes a magazine aimed specifically at trustees.

Children in Need (1999) *A Guide to Self-evaluation*
Charities Aid Foundation *Dimensions of the Voluntary Sector*

Appendix 2

Useful organizational contacts

The following is a list of some useful organizations. It is not intended to be an exhaustive list.

- Association of Chief Executives of Voluntary Organizations (ACEVO).
- Centre for Charity and Trust Research, South Bank University, London.
- Charities Aid Foundation (CAF). CAF provides a number of services. These include acting as an agency charity for payroll giving.
- Charity Commission. The Charity Commission has offices in London, Taunton and Liverpool. Visitors can use the commission database to research charities and charitable trusts, and can order 'public files' on any registered charity. The commission also publishes a range of booklets on charities and regulatory issues.
- Chartered Institute of Marketing (CIM). CIM is a membership organization that also runs the certificate, advanced certificate and diploma in marketing.
- Communications, Advertising and Marketing Foundation (CAM). CAM runs the CAM certificate and diploma in integrated marketing communications.
- Directory of Social Change (DSC). The DSC publishes a wide

range of materials, organizes courses and conferences and runs a meeting venue in central London.
▧ Give as You Earn (GAYE). GAYE is a payroll-giving scheme administered by the Charities Aid Foundation.
▧ Institute of Charity Fundraising Managers (ICFM). ICFM is a membership organization producing guidelines on standards, running courses and providing other services. Full membership is obtained through the certificate of fundraising management. Special interest groups cover issues like trust fundraising, technology and research.
▧ Institute of Public Relations (IPR). The IPR is a membership organization for those in PR. The special interest group for those in the voluntary sector is called Fifth Estate.
▧ Media Trust. The Media Trust aims to bring together experienced media staff and voluntary organizations. It runs conferences on a range of marketing related issues and maintains Web site discussion areas on many of these, including the issue of charity branding.
▧ National Council for Voluntary Organizations (NCVO). NCVO is a membership organization that provides services for charities while also acting as a voice for the sector. The organization runs a marketing forum and a PR forum. It also holds one-day conferences on a number of issues, including marketing.
▧ Scottish Council for Voluntary Organizations.
▧ South Bank University. South Bank University runs courses leading to qualifications in charity marketing, charity finance and other charity related topics.

Index

accidental givers   31
achievable PR targets   89
adverse publicity   85–86
advertising   84, 90, 148–55
    benefits and pitfalls   149–50
    finding out more   154–55
    options   150–54
'advertising features'   152
'advertising value equivalents'
    (AVEs)   124–25
advertorials   152
ambient media   153
American Express (Amex)   81
annual reports   110–18
    key points   117–18
    planning   113
    producing   114–17
arguments supporting core
    theme   139
audiences   145
    for live events   97–98,
    104–05
    for PR   86–87
AVEs (advertising value
    equivalents)   124–25

backbench MPs   37–38
Barnardo's   87, 146
'bespoke' database software
    162
'best of breed' database
    software   162
bookmarks   56–57
brand personality   8–9
branding   3, 7–17
    example   15–17
    importance   8–9
    names and logos   10–15
    re-branding   9–10
British Bobsleigh Association
    124
British Diabetic Association
    15–17
British Lung Foundation
    61
broadcast media advertising
    150–52
budgets
    for evaluation   123–24
    for live events   98
Burnett, K   59

calls to action 139
campaigning *see* lobbying
case histories 92, 144
case preparation for lobbying
    35–36
catering for live events 99–100
cause-related marketing (CRM)
    70–72, 81
celebrities 144
change management 163
changes of name, introducing
    13–15
changing environment of PR
    86
charitable trusts 31
charity sector, size of 1
chromalins 116
clients, PR partnerships with
    92
collaboration between charities
    93–94
colour printing 116
commissioning work 142
communications
    fitting Internet into objectives
        54
    further reading 168
    identifying goals 122
    integrated campaigning
        136
    with donors 61–62
communications mix 133–34
company donors 31, 68–83
    examples 80–83
    fundraising mix 69–74
    further reading 168
    new business development
        74–80
    reasons for working with
        charities 69

competition between charities
    93–94
conferences *see* events and
    conferences
consultants 21–24, 44–45
contact details on annual
    reports 117
context difficulties, Internet
    53–54
contractual considerations, live
    events 104
copy writing for annual reports
    115
core messages 138–39
corporate donations 73–74
corporate events 73
corporate fundraising mix
    69–74
costs of advertising 148, 149
counter-arguments 139
covers for annual reports
    117
creative design 134–35
Crisis 93–94, 137, 138–39,
    143
CRM *see* cause-related
    marketing
Cultural Trends 141
customers, meeting needs of
    1, 2

database marketing 156–65
    definition 157–58
    initial considerations 157,
        161–64
    key requirements 160–61
    value of 158–60
delegate management, live
    events 104–05
deliberate givers 31–32

design
  annual reports   114, 116, 117
  creative   134
devolved assemblies   38–39
Diabetes UK   15–17
digital media   120
direct marketing   58–59
  further reading   168
Disasters Emergency
  Committee   94, 150
disguised advertisements   152
'distress rates'   150
donors   3, 29–33
  communicating with   61–62
  companies   73–74
  individual   31–33
  organizations   31
  perceived as individual   61
  selecting groups to focus on
    63
  stakeholders   143
  thanking   62–63
  value of   61

editorial coverage   124, 125
'Eight Ps'   132–33
e-mails   51, 55
endorsement of campaigns
  144–45
entertaining politicians   43
EU institutions   39
evaluation techniques   119–28,
  147
  examples   126–28
  PR campaigns   89
events and conferences
  96–109
  corporate   73
  examples   105–08
  exhibitions   108–09

other considerations   103–05
  planning   97–103
exhibitions   108–09
external/internal consistency
  of campaigns   135

facilities management services
  161
FAQs (frequently asked
  questions)   51, 56
feedback   123
fees for membership clubs
  65–66
financial factors, integrated
  campaigning   135
focus groups   126
'Four Ps'   132
free advertisements   153–54
frequently asked questions
  (FAQs)   51, 56
Friends of the Earth   137

GANTT charts   141–42
guest books   56

Halifax Young Savers Account
  80–81
HAPs ('heightened awareness
  periods')   146
health and safety issues, live
  events   103–04
'heightened awareness periods'
  (HAPs)   146
home pages   57
horizontal integration   131–32
hostile questions   139
House of Lords   38

impact
  creating   144–45

sustaining 145–46
Indecent Exposure campaign
    90
Independent Television
    Commission (ITC)
    151–52
individual donors 31–33
ineffective campaigning
    43–44
insurance for live events 103
integrated campaigning
    42–43, 94, 129–47
  barriers to 135–36
  benefits 130
  definition 131–35
  management of 136–47
internal/external consistency
    of campaigns 135
Internet marketing 32–33,
    49–57, 94, 120–21
  characteristics 50, 53–54
  effective use 55
  further reading 168
  handling responses 51
  key words 56–57
  place in overall objectives
    54
  readers' behaviour 52–53
  reasons for 49–50
  research 56
investment levels, membership
    clubs 66
ITC *see* Independent Television
    Commission

Jeans for Genes campaign
    145
John Grooms charity 127–28
joining fees, membership clubs
    65

Key Performance Indicators
    72
Kotler 129
Kwik-Fit Insurance 81–83

laws on charities and politics
    40
  further reading 169
legal considerations, live events
    104
listings 152–53
live events *see* events and
    conferences
lobbying 34–45
  defining case 35–36
  effective 41–42
  further reading 167
  identifying targets 37–39
  ineffective 43–44
  integrated campaigning
    42–43
  potential PR conflict
    93–94
  timing and process 40
  using consultants 44–45
logos 10, 12–13

mailing lists 118
management support of
    campaigning 135
market research 125–26
marketing mix 132
mass mailings 43–44
measurement of results 123
'meat and two veg approach'
    88
media coverage 41, 84–85,
    120–21
  further reading 168
media partnerships 91

media tensions with PR 93
membership schemes 64–67
  further reading 168
monitoring political
    developments 40
MPs 37–38

names 10–12
navigation bars 57
navigational difficulties,
  Internet 53–54
NCH Action for Children
  19–20, 80–81, 82–83, 133
new business development
  74–80
Nichols, Judith 32, 33

objectives 121, 122
  live events 97
  PR 86–87
'old boy network' 43
open days 108
opinion formers, marketing to
  see lobbying
'opportunities to see' 149
organization donors 31
organizational structures
  18–26
  case history 19–20
  marketing to statutory sector
    24–26
  working with consultants
    21–24
outdoor advertising 153
ownership issues, integrated
  campaigning 136

parliament 37–39
parliamentary private
  secretaries (PPSs) 37

partnerships
  for PR campaigns 89–92
  with companies see company
    donors
passwords 57
payments to officials 43
payroll giving (PRG) 74,
  82–83
Peers 38
'People' criteria 133, 136
Peppers, D 59
'Philosophy' criteria 133
photographs for annual reports
  112, 114
'Physical evidence' criteria
  133
physically disabled
  requirements at live events
    100–01
'Place' criteria 132
planning strategies 21
  annual reports 113
  integrated campaigning
    135–36, 137–38
  live events 97–103
  PR strategies 86–89
  project 141–42
Policy Unit members 37
political communications see
  lobbying
political contact audits 39
positioning 3, 88
PR see public relations
presentations at live events
  101–02
PRG see payroll giving
'Price' criteria 132
print media advertising 150
print process, annual reports
  116–17

printing Internet information
54
privatization, effects of 24
pro bono advertising 90
'Process' criteria 133
'Product' criteria 132, 136
production processes, annual
reports 115–17
project plans 141–42
project teams 139–40, 146–47
'Promotion' criteria 132–33
public affairs tension with PR
92–93
public relations (PR) 84–95
further reading 168
natural tensions 92–94
partnerships 89–92
planning 86–89

qualitative research 126
quantitative research 126

radio advertising 150–52
Radio Authority 151
reactive public relations work
85
readers' behaviour, Internet
52–53
reading recommendations
166–69
re-branding 9–10
recruitment advertising 154
Regional Development
Agencies 38–39
regional media coverage
91–92
relationship marketing 58–63,
67
communicating with donors
61–62

further reading 168
getting started 59–60
seeing donors as individuals
61
selecting groups to focus on
63
'thank yous' 62–63
value of donors 61
repeat visits to Web sites,
encouraging 55
repetition in advertising
149–50
reports *see* annual reports
research 125–26
integrated campaigning 144
new business development
76
re-branding 9–10
Web sites 56
resources
integrated campaigning
142
live events 98
PR 87
response handling, Internet
marketing 51
risk strategies in PR 85–86
RNIB (Royal National Institute
for the Blind) 146
RNID (Royal National Institute
for Deaf People) 90
RNLI (Royal National
Lifeboat Institution) 121,
126–27
Rogers, M 59
'round robin' letters 76
Royal National Institute for
Deaf People (RNID) 90
Royal National Institute for the
Blind (RNIB) 146

Royal National Lifeboat
    Institution (RNLI)   121,
    126–27
Royal Society for the
    Prevention of Cruelty to
    Animals (RSPCA)
    42–43

safety issues, live events
    103–04
Save the Children   87, 153
Scope conference case study
    105–07
'scorecard' comparisons   163
screen/projection presentations
    101–02
search engines   57
seating for live events   99
Shelter   87, 89, 90, 91,
    93–94
'short and dirty' PR hits   89
shrink-wrapped database
    packages   161, 164
small organizations   21, 165
societies that are donors   31
sound systems for live events
    102
speakers' technical facilities for
    live events   102–03
special advisers (to
    government)   37
special needs requirements at
    live events   100–01
sponsorship   73
staff as stakeholders   143
staff fundraising   69–70
stages and sets for live events
    102, 103
stakeholders of integrated
    campaigning   143

statements of requirements,
    and database choice
    162–63
statutory sector, marketing to
    24–26
    further reading   166
strategies for PR campaigns
    88
Strip 4 Shelter   91
structured fact finds   163
Sun, The   91
'surfing the Net'   57
surveys   126

targets
    lobbying   37–39
    public relations   86–87
technical services, live events
    101–03
test loadings of database
    software   163
thanking donors   62–63
themes for live events   98
timing   145
    lobbying   40
    membership schemes
    66–67
TV advertising   150–52

UK Offshore Operators
    Association Limited
    (UKOOA)   90
URLs   57
useful organizations   170–71

venue-finding agencies   104
venues for live events   98–99,
    145
vertical integration   131
visual identity changes   10–15

volunteers as stakeholders
  143

Web sites *see* Internet
  marketing

'wet proofs'　116
workability of names　11–12
World Wide Web *see* Internet
  marketing
www　57